PERGAMON INTERNA  **S0-BNU-102**

of Science, Technology, Engineering and Social Studies

*The 1000-volume original paperback library in aid of education,
industrial training and the enjoyment of leisure*

Publisher: Robert Maxwell, M.C.

SPANISH–ENGLISH/ENGLISH–SPANISH
COMMERCIAL DICTIONARY

DICCIONARIO DE COMERCIO
ESPAÑOL–INGLES/INGLES–ESPAÑOL

THE PERGAMON TEXTBOOK
INSPECTION COPY SERVICE

SPANISH–ENGLISH/ENGLISH–SPANISH
COMMERCIAL DICTIONARY

DICCIONARIO DE COMERCIO
ESPAÑOL–INGLES/INGLES–ESPAÑOL

BY

CARLOS REYES OROZCO
Universidad Nacional Autónoma de México

PERGAMON PRESS

OXFORD · NEW YORK · TORONTO · SYDNEY
PARIS · FRANKFURT

U.K.	Pergamon Press Ltd, Headington Hill Hall, Oxford OX3 0BW, England
U.S.A.	Pergamon Press Inc., Maxwell House, Fairview Park, Elmsford, New York 10523, U.S.A.
CANADA	Pergamon of Canada Ltd., 75 The East Mall, Toronto, Ontario, Canada
AUSTRALIA	Pergamon Press (Aust.) Pty. Ltd., 19a Boundary Street, Rushcutters Bay, N.S.W. 2011, Australia
FRANCE	Pergamon Press SARL, 24 rue des Ecoles, 75240 Paris, Cedex 05 France
FEDERAL REPUBLIC OF GERMANY	Pergamon Press GmbH, 6242 Kronberg-Taunus, Pferdstrasse 1, Federal Republic of Germany

First edition 1969
Reprinted 1978

Library of Congress Catalog Card No. 70–78905

Printed Offset Litho in Great Britain by Cox & Wyman Ltd, Fakenham, Norfolk
ISBN 0 08 006380 2

Contents

Foreword

IN THE last twenty years international trade has substantially increased in all English- and Spanish-speaking countries. This has resulted in a marked evolution of technical vocabulary.

The purpose of this glossary of commercial and economic terms is to supplement existing English and Spanish dictionaries. It is designed to serve the needs of businessmen, exporters and importers, economists, bankers, accountants and translators, as well as schools of commerce and economics. I hope that for all of them this technical dictionary will be a useful reference book in their sphere of activity.

Any comments and suggestions, to bear in mind for future editions, will be received with genuine appreciation.

C. REYES OROZCO

Prólogo

LA RÁPIDA evolución económica que ha habido en los últimos veinte años, en los países de habla inglesa y española, ha dado lugar a una evolución también muy notable en el vocabulario técnico.

Este diccionario ha sido preparado con el fin de presentar los vocablos propios del comercio y la economía que no se encuentren en los diccionarios ordinarios. Está especialmente dedicado a los empresarios, economistas, exportadores e importadores, banqueros, contadores y traductores, así como a las escuelas de comercio y economía. Espero que esta obra de consulta sea, para todos ellos, de gran utilidad.

Toda sugerencia acerca de este diccionario será recibida con genuino agradecimiento.

CARLOS REYES OROZCO

Spanish–English
Español–Inglés

A

abandono, abandonment.

abaratar, to lower the price.

abarcar, to cover, to include.

abarrotado, congested, jammed.

— **de mercancías,** overstocked.

abastecedor, supplier.

abastecer, to furnish, to supply.

abastecimientos, supplies, stock.

abatimiento del mercado, slackness of the market.

abatir, to lower.

abogado, attorney, lawyer.

abogar, to advocate.

abolir, to revoke, to annul.

abonable, payable.

abonado, subscriber.

abonar, to credit.

— **a la cuenta,** to credit the account.

abono, credit entry, installment.

abrir, to open.

— **propuestas,** to open bids.

— **un crédito,** to open a credit.

— **una cuenta,** to open an account.

abrogar, to annul, to repeal.

absentismo, absenteeism.

absoluto, absolute.

—**, endoso,** absolute endorsement.

absorber la pérdida, to absorb the loss.

acaparador, monopolist, profiteer.

acaparamiento, monopoly.

acaparar, to monopolize, to hoard.

— **el mercado,** to corner the market.

acarrear, to transport, to carry.

acarreo, cartage, transportation.

accidente de trabajo, industrial accident, occupational injury.

acción, action, share of stock.

— **hipotecaria,** foreclosure.

acciones, shares of stock.

— **acumulativas,** cumulative stock.

— **al portador,** bearer shares.

— **autorizadas,** authorized stock.

— **comunes,** common stock.

— **con derecho de voto,** voting stock.

— **cubiertas,** full-paid shares.

— **de administración,** management stock.

— **de capital,** capital stock.

— **de fundador,** founders' shares.

— **de voto plural,** plural-voting stock.

— **diferidas,** deferred stock.

— **emitidas,** issued stock.

— **en circulación,** outstanding stock.

— **exhibidas,** full-paid shares.

— **inscritas,** listed stocks.

— **ordinarias,** common stock, equities.

— **preferentes,** preferred stock.

— **preferentes participantes,** participating stock.

— **preferidas,** preferred stock.

— **primitivas,** original stock.

— **privilegiadas,** preferred stock.

— **sin derecho a voto,** nonvoting stock.

— **sin valor nominal,** non-par-value stock.

— **suscritas,** subscribed capital stock.

accionista, stockholder, shareholder.

accionistas, stockholders.

— **consencientes,** assenting stockholders.

— **disidentes,** nonassenting stockholders.

aceptación, acceptance.

— **bancaria,** bank acceptance.

— **commercial,** trade acceptance.

— **condicionada,** qualified acceptance.

— **contra documentos,** acceptance against documents.

— **de favor,** accommodation acceptance.

— **sin reservas,** general acceptance.

aceptar, to accept, to honor.

acre, acre.

acreditar, to authorize, to credit.

acreedor, creditor.

— **hipotecario,** mortgagee.

— **ordinario,** general creditor.

— **privilegiado,** preferred creditor.

acreedores diversos, sundry creditors.

actas, minutes of a meeting.

activo, active assets.

— **acumulado,** acrued assets.

— **aparente,** intangible assets.

— **circulante,** circulating assets, working assets.

— **comercial,** current assets.

— **diferido,** deferred assets.

— **disponible,** liquid assets, funds available, cash in hand.

— **dudoso,** doubtful assets.

— **en divisas,** foreign-exchange assets.

— **fijo,** capital assets, fixed capital.

— **intangible,** intangibles.

— **líquido,** net worth.

— **neto,** net worth.

— **oculto,** concealed assets.

— **permanente,** permanent assets.

— **tangible,** tangible assets.

— **y pasivo,** assets and liabilities.

activos, assets.

— **comprometidos,** committed assets.

— **sociales,** corporate assets.

acto mercantil, commercial transaction.

actual, current, present.

actuario, actuary.

acuerdo, agreement, resolution.

— **comercial de reciprocidad,** reciprocal trade agreement.

— **comercial de intercambio,** trade agreement.

— **de compensación,** clearing agreement.

— **por escrito,** written agreement.

acumulable, cumulative, accumulative.

acumulaciones, accruals.

acumular, to accrue.

acumulativo, cumulative.

acuñar moneda, to mint.

acusar recibo, to acknowledge receipt.

acuse de recibo, acknowledge receipt.

adelantado, por, in advance.

adelantar, to pay in advance.

adelanto, advance.

— **sobre valores,** advance upon collateral (security).

adeudar, to owe, to debit.

adeudo, indebtedness, debit.

adición, addition.

adicionar, to add.

adiestramiento, training.

adiestrar, to train.

adinerado, wealthy.

adjudicación, award, adjudication.

adjuntar, to attach, to enclose.

administración, administration, management.

administrar, to manage, to administer.

administrativo, administrative, executive.

adquirir, to acquire.

adquisición, acquisition.

adquisitivo, poder, purchasing power.

aduana, customhouse.

—, **aranceles de,** customs tariffs.

—, **derechos de,** customs duties.

—, **exento de derechos de,** customs-exempt.

—, **fianza de,** customs bond.

—, **ingresos de,** customs receipts.

—, **manifiesto de,** customs manifest.

afianzable, bondable.

afianzado, bonded.

afiliada, affiliated.

afiliar, to affiliate.

afluencia de capitales, inflow of capital.

agencia, agency, bureau.

— **de colocaciones,** employment agency.

agente, agent.

— **de aduana,** customhouse broker, forwarding agent.

— **de bolsa,** stockbroker.

— **de negocios,** business agent.

— **de seguros,** insurance broker.

— **de ventas,** sales agent.

— **viajero,** traveling salesman, commercial traveler.

agio, usury, speculation.

agiotaje, usury, speculation.

agiotista, usurer, speculator.

agotado, out-of-stock.

agotamiento, depletion.

agotar, to deplete.

agregar, to add.

ahorrar, to save, to economize.

ahorro, saving, economy.

— **negativo,** dissaving.

ajustador, adjuster.

— **de derechos,** customs appraiser.

— **de seguros,** insurance claim adjuster.

ajustar, to adjust, to settle.

ajuste, adjustment, settlement.

— **automático de sueldos,** automatic wage adjustment.

al azar, at random.

—, **muestra,** random sample.

albacea, executor.

alcista, bull, bullish.

aleatorio, random.

—, **comienzo,** random start.

—, **error del muestreo,** random sampling error.

aleatorización, randomization.

— **restringida,** restricted randomization.

aliciente, incentive.

alienar, to alienate.

alimentar, to feed.

almacén, store, stock room, warehouse.

—, **en,** in stock.

almacenaje, storage.

almacenar, to store.

almoneda, auction.

alquilar, to rent.

6

alquiler, rent.
altas finanzas, high finance.
alto funcionario, high official.
alto rendimiento, high yield.
alza, rise.
— **de impuestos,** increase of taxes.
— **de salarios,** raise of wages.
alzar el precio, to raise the price.
amarraje, berthage.
aminorar, to reduce.
amistoso, friendly.
amonedar, to coin.
amortizable, amortizable, redeemable.
amortización, amortization, redemption.
— **constante,** straight-line depreciation.
— **de una deuda,** debt redemption.
amortizar, to amortize, to redeem.
— **una deuda,** to sink a debt.
amplitud del error prescrito, prescribed range of error.
análisis, analysis.
— **de grupos humanos,** cohort analysis.
— **de mercados,** market research.
anexo, enclosure.
animar el comercio, to stimulate trade.

anotar un pedido, to book an order.
antedicho, above mentioned.
antefechar, to antedate, foredate.
antefirma, title before signature.
antes mencionado, abovementioned.
anticipación, con, in advance.
anticipadamente, in advance.
anticipar, to advance (money).
anticipo, advance payment.
anticipos reembolsables, returnable advances.
antieconómico, uneconomic.
antigüedad, seniority.
antimonopolista, antimonopoly.
antimonopolístico, antitrust.
antítesis cronológica, time antithesis.
anual, annual, yearly.
anualidad, annuity.
— **acumulada,** accumulated annuity.
— **completa,** complete annuity.
— **diferida,** deferred annuity.
— **pasiva,** annuity payable.
— **vitalicia,** life annuity.
anualmente, annually, yearly.
anular, to annul, to cancel, to invalidate.
anuncio, advertisement.

año, year.

— **comercial,** commercial year.

— **fiscal,** fiscal year.

— **magro,** lean year.

apelación, appeal.

apelar, to appeal.

aplazar, to defer, to postpone.

aplicable, applicable.

aplicar, to apply, to allocate.

— **impuestos,** to impose taxes.

apoderado, empowered, authorized, proxy, attorney.

aportación, contribution.

aportaciones en especie, assets in kind.

aportar fondos, to finance.

apoyar, to support, to back.

apoyo financiero, financial backing.

apreciación, appraisal, rating.

— **preferida,** preferred rating.

apreciar, to appraise, to value.

aprecio, appraisal, valuation.

apresurar, to expedite.

aprobación, approval, authorization.

aprobar, to approve, to pass.

apropiar, to assign, to allocate.

aprovechable, usable.

arancel, tariff.

— **de exportación,** duties on exports.

— **diferencial,** differential duties.

— **fiscal,** revenue tariff.

— **proteccionista,** protective tariff.

arbitración, arbitration.

arbitraje, arbitration.

— **de cambio,** arbitration (of) exchange.

archivar, to file letters.

archivista, file clerk.

archivo, (office) file.

aritmética, arithmetic.

arqueo, audit, appraisal of assets, cash count.

arreglar una cuenta, to settle an account.

arrendador, lessor, landlord.

arrendamiento, lease, rent.

arrendar, to lease, to let, to rent.

arrendatario, tenant, lessee.

arriendo, rental, lease.

artículos, goods, products.

— **de consumo,** consumer goods.

— **de exportación,** export commodities, export goods.

— **de importación,** import goods.

— **de lujo,** luxuries.

— **de primera necesidad,** primary wants.

— **y servicios,** goods and services.

asalariado, wage earner.

asamblea, meeting.

asegurable, insurable.

asegurado, insured, covered.

asegurador, insurer.

aseguradores, underwriters.

— contra riesgos marítimos, marine underwriters.

asentar, to enter.

— una partida, to make an entry.

asesor, adviser.

— comercial, business counselor.

— económico, financial adviser.

— sobre administración, management consultant.

asesorar, to advise.

asiento, entry.

— confuso, blind entry.

— cruzado, cross entry.

— de abono, credit entry.

— de apertura, opening entry.

— de caja, cash entry, cash item.

— de cargo, debit entry.

— de crédito, credit entry.

— de débito, debit item.

— de diario, journal entry.

— de traspaso, transfer entry.

— del mayor, ledger entry.

asignación, allotment, assignment, allocation.

asignar, to allocate, to assign, to allot.

— fondos a . . . , to appropriate funds to. . . .

— las acciones integralmente, to allot the shares in full.

asintótico, asymtotical.

asistencia, assistance, relief.

— pública, public welfare work.

— social, relief, social welfare.

— técnica, technical assistance.

asociación, association, company.

asociado, associate, partner.

asociarse, to form a partnership.

asumir la pérdida, to absorb the loss.

asunto, matter, business, subject.

atender, to take care of, to handle.

atraer clientela, to attract customers.

atrasado, late, delinquent.

atrasarse, to be late, to be in arrears.

atraso, delay.

atrasos, arrears.

auditar, to audit.

auditor, auditor.

auditoría, audit, auditing.

— de balance, balance-sheet audit.

— de caja, cash audit.

— interna, internal audit.

— **parcial,** partial audit.

— **privada,** internal audit.

— **pública,** public audit.

auge, peak, boom.

— **económico,** prosperity.

aumentar, to increase.

aumento, increase.

— **de demanda,** pick-up demand.

— **de precio,** increased price.

— **de sueldo,** raise in salary.

— **medio anual,** average annual increase.

ausentismo, absenteeism.

auspiciar, to sponsor, to back.

auténtico, authentic, certified.

autoconsumo, self-consumption.

automático, automatic.

automatismo, automation.

automatizar, to automatize.

autonomía, autonomy.

— **económica,** economic self-sufficiency.

autónomo, autonomous.

autoridad, authority.

autoridades portuarias, port authorities.

autorización, authorization.

— **global,** over-all authorization.

autorizado, authorized.

autorizar, to authorize, empower.

autosuficiencia, selt-sufficiency.

autosuficiente, self-sufficient.

auxiliar, assistant, auxiliary.

— **de caja,** auxiliary cashbook.

— **del gerente,** assistant manager.

— **del mayor,** auxiliary ledger.

aval, endorsement.

— **absoluto,** full endorsement.

— **limitado,** qualified endorsement.

avalar, to endorse, to back.

avalúo, appraisal, valuation, evaluation.

— **catastral,** assessed valuation.

— **fiscal,** appraisal for taxation.

avenencia, compromise, deal.

avenimiento, agreement.

avería, damage, average.

— **gruesa,** gross average.

— **menor,** petty average.

avisar, to notify, to advise.

aviso, advice, notice.

— **de embarque,** shipping notice.

— **de llegada,** arrival notice.

— **de protesto,** notice of protest.

ayuda, assistance, aid.

— **mutua,** mutual assistance.

— **no selectiva,** nondiscriminatory assistance.

ayudante, assistant.

10

— **administrador,** assistant manager.

— **cajero,** assistant cashier.

ayudar, to help, to assist.

azar, risk, accident.

—, **al,** at random.

B

bagaje, baggage.

baja, fall, drop, decline.

— **del mercado,** drop of prices.

— **económica,** business depression.

— **violenta,** crash (stock exchange).

bajar de valor, to decline in value.

bajista, bear, bearish.

bajo, low, below, under.

— **contrato,** under contract.

— **fianza,** under bond.

— **par,** below par.

balance, balance, balance sheet.

— **analítico,** analytical balance sheet.

— **bancario,** statement of condition.

— **comparativo,** comparative statement.

— **consolidado,** consolidated balance sheet.

— **de comprobación,** trial balance.

— **de operación,** profit and loss statement.

— **del banco,** bank statement.

— **del mayor,** ledger balance.

—, **en,** in balance.

— **tentativo,** tentative balance sheet.

balancear, to balance.

— **el presupuesto,** to balance the budget.

balanza, balance.

— **comercial,** balance of trade.

— **comercial desfavorable,** adverse trade balance.

— **de cambios,** balance of trade.

— **de comprobación,** trial balance.

— **de pagos al exterior,** balance of external payments.

— **de pagos negativa,** unfavorable balance of payments.

— **de pagos positiva,** favorable balance of payments.

— **de prueba,** trial balance.

— **económica,** balance of international payments.

— **visible de comercio,** visible balance of trade.

banca, banking.

11

— **central,** central banking.

— **privada,** private banking.

bancarrota, bankruptcy.

banco, bank.

— **de ahorros,** savings bank.

— **de descuento,** discount bank, commercial bank.

— **de fomento,** development bank.

— **del estado,** government bank.

— **emisor,** bank of issue.

— **estatal,** government bank.

— **fiduciario,** trust company.

— **hipotecario,** mortgage bank.

— **no respaldado,** nonmember bank.

barata, bargain, bargain sale.

barra de abogados, bar association.

barrera, barrier.

barreras, barriers.

— **arancelarias,** tariff barriers.

— **comerciales,** trade barriers.

báscula, scale.

base, base, basis.

— **acumulativa,** accrual basis.

— **de avalúo,** basis of assessment.

— **de depreciación,** basis for depreciation.

— **impositiva,** tax base.

beneficencia, social service, welfare.

beneficiado, beneficiary.

beneficiario, beneficiary.

beneficio, gain, profit, benefit.

— **justo,** fair return.

beneficios no retribuídos, retained earning.

beneficioso, profitable.

bias, bias.

bienes, property, assets.

— **capitales,** capital goods.

— **circulantes,** circulating assets.

— **comerciales,** stock in trade.

— **de consumo,** consumer goods.

— **de producción,** producer's goods.

— **durables,** durable goods.

— **inmuebles,** real estate.

— **materiales,** material goods.

— **muebles,** movables, chattels.

— **no duraderos,** nondurable goods.

— **raíces,** immovables.

— **y servicios,** goods and services.

bienestar social, social welfare.

billete, bill.

— **de banco,** bank note.

billón (un millón de millones), (U.K. = billion) (U.S.A. = 1000 millions).

bimestral, bimonthly.
bimestre, two months.
bimetalismo, bimetallism, double standard.
bloque, block.
bloquear, to freeze funds.
bloques aleatorizados, randomized blocks.
boicot, boycott.
boicotear, to boycott.
boleta, ticket.
— de pago predial, real-estate tax receipt.
bolsa de valores, stock exchange.
bonanza, prosperity.
bonificación, bonus, allowance.
— tributaria, tax rebate.
bonificaciones sobre ventas, sales discounts.
bonificar, to credit.
bono, bond, bonus.
— de plazo largo, long-term bond.
— de rendimiento bajo, low-yield bond.

— del estado, government bond, state bond.
— hipotecario, mortgage bond.
— inmobiliario, real-estate bond.
— no transferible, restricted bond.
— nominal, registered bond.
— privilegiado, priority bond.
— redimible, callable bond.
— sin garantía hipotecaria, debenture bond.
bonos, bonds.
— al portador, coupon bonds.
— de amortización, sinking-fund bonds.
bordo, a, on board.
borrador, rough draft, daybook.
bruto, gross, in bulk.
buenos oficios, good offices.
bufete jurídico, lawyer's office.
bulto, package, parcel.
buró, agency, bureau.
burocracia, bureaucracy.
burócrata, bureaucrat.

C

cablegrafiar, to send a cable.
cabotaje, coastwise shipping.
caducar, to expire.
caja, safe, cashier's office.

— chica, petty cash.
— de ahorros, savings bank.
— de amortización, sinking fund.
— de caudales, safe.

— **de seguridad,** safe-deposit box.

— **registradora,** cash register.

cajero, cashier, teller.

— **menor,** petty cashier.

— **principal,** head teller.

— **recibidor,** receiving teller.

calculadora, computer.

— **digital,** digital computer.

calcular, to compute, to figure.

calculista, estimator, calculator.

cálculo, estimate, calculus.

calidad, quality, grade.

calificación, qualification, rating.

— **fiscal,** assessment.

calificado, qualified, competent.

cámara, chamber, board.

— **de comercio,** chamber of commerce.

cambiable, exchangeable.

cambiar, to change, to cash, to exchange.

— **cheques,** to cash checks.

— **una letra,** to negotiate a bill.

cambio, change, exchange, rate of exchange.

— **a la par,** exchange at par.

— **de cierre,** closing rate of exchange.

— **del día,** spot exchange.

— **oficial,** official rate of exchange.

campo, field, country

— **de actividad,** field of activity.

cancelación, cancellation, annulment, payment.

— **de una deuda,** discharge of a debt.

cancelar, to cancel, to liquidate.

— **una deuda,** to wipe off a debt.

cancillería, ministry of foreign affairs.

canje, conversion, trade-in.

canjeable, convertible.

canjear, to convert.

cantidad, quantity, amount.

cantidades sobrevencidas, amounts past due.

capacidad, capacity, ability.

— **adquisitiva,** purchasing power.

— **contributiva individual,** individual tax-paying capacity.

— **crediticia,** lending capacity.

— **de pago,** ability to pay.

— **de producción,** plant capacity.

— **económica,** financial standing.

capaz, competent, able.

capitación, head tax.

capital, capital.

— **activo,** working capital.

—, **afluencia de,** capital inflow.

— **aportado,** invested capital.

— **autorizado,** authorized capital.

— **circulante,** circulating capital.

— **de operación,** working capital.

— **de producción,** producers' capital.

— **declarado,** declared capital.

— **exhibido,** paid-in capital.

— **emitido,** issued capital.

— **inflado,** watered stock.

— **inicial,** original capital.

— **invertido,** invested capital.

— **neto,** net worth.

— **real,** capital assets.

— **social,** capital stock.

— **subscrito,** subscribed capital.

capitalismo, capitalism.

capitalista, capitalist, capitalistic investor.

capitalización, capitalization.

— **de intereses,** compounding of interest.

capitalizar, to capitalize.

carga, load, freight, cargo.

— **a granel,** bulk cargo.

— **aérea,** air freight.

— **marítima,** cargo, ocean freight.

— **muerta,** dead load.

— **seca,** dry cargo.

cargado, loaded.

cargamento, load, cargo.

— **completo,** full load.

cargar a la cuenta, to debit the account.

cargo, job, position, debit.

— **administrativo,** executive position.

— **por cobro,** collection charge.

— **y abono,** debit and credit.

cargos, charges.

— **bancarios,** bank charges.

— **diferidos,** deferred charges.

— **fijos,** fixed charges.

carpeta, folder.

carta, letter, charter, map.

— **aérea,** air-mail letter.

— **blanca,** carte blanche, full power.

— **certificada,** registered letter.

— **comercial de crédito,** commercial letter of credit.

— **constitutiva,** corporation charter.

— **de crédito,** letter of credit.

— **de crédito irrevocable,** irrevocable letter of credit.

— **de entrega inmediata,** special-delivery letter.

— **de presentación,** letter of introduction.

— **de recomendación,** letter of recommendation.

— **marina,** chart, ocean chart.

15

— **poder,** proxy, power of attorney.

cartel, cartel, combine.

— **de precios,** cartel for price fixing.

— **regional,** regional cartel.

cartelización, cartelization.

cartera, portfolio, list of securities owned.

— **bancaria,** list of bills discounted.

—**, en,** on hand.

casa, house, firm, concern, company.

— **de moneda,** mint.

— **matriz,** parent house.

casilla de correo, post-office box.

catalogar, to catalogue, to list.

catálogo, catalogue, list.

— **de cuentas,** list of accounts.

catastro, real-estate register, cadastre.

categoría, category, quality, rank.

caución, guarantee, security.

causa, cause, case, lawsuit.

causante moroso, delinquent taxpayer.

causar impuesto, to be subject to tax.

cédula, official document.

— **fiscal,** form for income-tax return.

— **hipotecaria,** mortgage-bond.

celebrar un contrato, to enter into a contract.

censar, to take a census.

censo, census.

— **de distribución,** distribution census.

centena, hundred.

centigramo (cg), centigram (0.1543 grain (avdp.)).

centilitro (cl), centiliter (0.3381 fl. oz.).

centímetro (cm), centimeter (0.3937 in.).

centro de ubicación, center of location.

centro comercial, shopping center.

cerrar la cuenta, to close the account.

certificado, certificate.

— **con salvedades,** qualified certificate.

— **consular,** consular certificate.

— **de acciones,** stock certificate.

— **de adeudo,** indebtedness certificate.

— **de auditoría,** audit certificate.

— **de depósito,** certificate of deposit.

— **de fabricación,** certificate of manufacture.

— **de orígen,** certificate of origin.

certificar, to certify.
cesante, unemployed.
cesar, to cease, to stop, to discharge.
cese, layoff, dismissal.
cibernética, cybernetics.
cíclico, cyclic.
ciclo económico, economic cycle.
cierre, closing.
— **anterior,** previous close.
— **de cuentas,** closing of accounts.
— **de los libros,** closing the books.
cifra, figure, number.
— **global,** lump sum.
cifras ajustadas, adjusted figures.
cifrado, in code.
cinta, tape, ribbon.
— **de máquina,** typewriter ribbon.
— **del indicador eléctrico,** ticker tape.
circulante, circulating, current.
circular, (carta), form letter.
círculos financieros, financial circles.
circunstancias financieras, financial condition.
cita, appointment.
— **previa, con,** by appointment.

citar a junta, to call a meeting.
clase, class, grade.
clases mutuamente excluyentes, mutually exclusive classes.
clasificable, classifiable.
clasificación, classification.
— **del trabajo por su calidad,** job evaluation.
clasificado para crédito, rated.
clasificar, to classify, to grade.
cláusula, clause.
— **adicional,** rider.
— **de escape,** escape clause.
— **de exclusión,** exclusion clause, closed-shop provision.
— **de la nación más favorecida,** most favored-nation clause.
— **de punto crítico,** peril point clause.
— **penal,** penalty clause.
clausura, closing, closure.
— **de los libros,** closing the books.
— **de sesiones,** adjournment.
clausurar, to close, to adjourn.
clave, code, key.
— **comercial,** commercial code.
cliente, customer, account.
— **en perspectiva,** prospective customer.

clientela, clientele, customers.
coacreedor, cocreditor.
coadministrador, coadministrator.
coalición, association, coalition.
coasegurado, coinsured.
coasociación, partnership, co-partnership.
cobertura, cover.
cobrabilidad, collectibility.
cobrable, collectible.
cobrador, collector.
cobranza, collection.
cobrar, to collect.
— **a la entrega,** to collect on delivery.
— **de más,** to overcharge.
cóbrese al entregar, collect on delivery (C.O.D.).
cobro, al, for collection.
— **directo,** direct collection.
— **por adelantado,** advanced collections.
codeudor, co-debtor.
codeudores, joint debtors.
codificar, to code, to codify.
código, code.
— **de comercio,** commercial code.
— **de ética,** code of ethics.
— **de quiebras,** bankruptcy law.
— **del trabajo,** labor laws.
— **fiscal,** tax laws.

— **mercantil,** commercial law.
coeficiente, coefficient, factor.
— **de amortización,** amortization factor.
— **de elasticidad,** coefficient of elasticity.
— **de liquidez,** current ratio.
— **de mortalidad,** death rate.
— **de natalidad,** birth rate.
— **de repartición,** coefficient of apportionment.
— **de seguridad,** factor of safety.
— **de variación,** coefficient of variation.
— **insumo producto,** input-output coefficient.
cofirmante, cosigner.
cogirador, codrawer.
cohechar, to bribe.
cohecho, bribe, bribery.
coherederos, joint heirs.
colapso, collapse.
colateral, collateral.
colección, collection.
colectar, to collect.
colector de rentas, collector of internal revenue.
colegio de corredores, brokers' association.
colisión, collision.
colocación, position, employment.
colocar, to place.
— **a interés,** to place at interest.

— **dinero,** to invest money.

— **un empréstito,** to place a loan.

— **un pedido,** to place an order.

comandita, silent partnership.

— **por acciones,** stock association.

comanditado, active partner.

comanditario, silent partner.

combinación de errores, pooling of errors.

combinar, to combine, to merge.

comerciabilidad, marketability.

comerciable, marketable.

comercial, commercial.

comercializar, to commercialize, to market.

comerciante, merchant, businessman.

— **al por mayor,** wholesaler.

— **al por menor,** retailer.

— **comisionista,** commission merchant.

comercio, commerce, trade, business.

— **al menudeo,** retail trade.

— **al por mayor,** wholesale trade.

— **de cabotaje,** coastwise trade.

— **exterior,** foreign trade, export trade.

— **interestatal,** interstate commerce.

— **interior,** domestic trade.

— **invisible,** invisible trade.

— **libre,** free trade.

comisión, commission.

—, **a,** on commission.

— **consultiva,** advisory commission.

—, **en,** on commission.

— **mixta,** joint committee.

comisionar, to commission.

comisionista, commission merchant, broker.

— **de acciones,** stockbroker.

comité, committee.

— **administrativo,** executive committee.

— **ejecutivo,** executive committee.

compañía, company, corporation.

— **anónima,** stock company.

— **bancaria,** banking company.

— **de seguros,** insurance company.

— **filial,** affiliated company.

— **fusionada,** merged company.

— **inactiva,** non-operating company.

— **inmobiliaria,** real-estate company.

— **matriz,** parent company, holding company.

— **por acciones,** stock company.

compañías afines, related companies.

comparación macroeconómica, macro-economic comparison.

comparaciones entre países, inter-country comparisons.

compensable, balancing, equalizing.

compensación, compensation.

— **obligatoria,** compulsory compensation.

compensaciones bancarias, bank clearings.

compensar, to clear.

compensatorio, countervailing.

competencia, competition.

— **extranjera,** foreign competition.

— **injusta,** unfair competition.

competente, competent, capable.

complementario, complementary.

complemento, complement.

comportamiento de los precios, price behavior.

compra, purchase, buying.

— **a plazos,** installment buying, hire purchase.

— **para cubrir ventas al descubierto,** short covering.

comprador, buyer.

comprar, to buy.

— **a crédito,** to buy on credit.

— **al por mayor,** to buy at wholesale.

— **con rebaja,** to buy at a discount.

compras en abonos, installment buying.

comprobante, voucher.

— **de caja chica,** petty-cash voucher.

— **de gastos,** expense voucher.

— **de pago,** receipt.

— **de retiro de fondos,** withdrawal voucher.

— **de venta,** bill of sale.

comprobar, to check, to verify.

compuesto, compound.

computable, computable.

computador, computer.

— **electrónico (digital),** digital computer.

computar, to compute, to calculate.

con dividendo incluído, cum dividend.

conceder, to grant, to allow.

— **crédito,** to extend credit.

— **interés,** to allow interest.

— **un descuento,** to allow a discount.

— **un préstamo,** to make a loan.

concejo, council, board.

— **municipal,** city council.

concentración, recapitulation.

concepto, concept, item.

conceptos, particulars.

concertar un contrato, to make a contract.

concesión, concession, franchise, grant.

— **arancelaria,** tariff concession.

concesionario, concessionaire, licensee.

conciliar, to conciliate.

— **las cuentas,** to reconcile accounts.

condicionado, qualified.

condiciones

— **de crédito,** credit terms.

— **de pago,** terms of sale.

— **de venta,** sales terms.

condominio, joint ownership.

conferencia, conference, syndicate, lecture.

— **marítima,** shipping conference.

conferir, to confer, to consult.

— **poderes,** to empower.

confiabilidad, reliability.

confiable, reliable, dependable.

confianza, confidence, trust.

confirmación, confirmation, acknowledgment.

confirmar, to confirm, to ratify.

confiscar, to seize, to expropriate.

conflicto, dispute.

congelación de fondos, blocking of funds.

congelado, frozen.

conocimiento de embarque, bill of lading.

consejero, adviser, consultant.

consejo, commission, board, councel, advice.

— **consultivo,** consulting board.

— **directivo,** board of directors.

conservación, maintenance.

— **de suelos,** soil conservation.

conservar, to maintain, to keep.

consignación, a, on consignment.

consignar, to consign.

consignatario, consignee.

consolidable, fundable.

consolidación, consolidation.

consolidado, funded.

consolidar, to consolidate.

consorcio, consortium, syndicate.

constituir, to establish, to organize.

consultor economista, economic adviser.

consumidor-comprador, consumer-purchaser.

consumir, to consume.

consumo, consumption.

—, **artículos de,** consumption-goods.

—, **función,** consumption-function.

— **interno,** domestic consumption.

contabilidad, accounting, bookkeeping.

— **de costos,** cost accounting.

— **de partida doble,** double-entry bookkeeping.

— **de partida simple,** single-entry bookkeeping.

— **de sociedades,** corporation accounting.

— **de sucesiones,** estate accounting.

— **fiscal,** government accounting.

contabilización, journalizing.

contabilizar, to journalize.

contable, (*adj.*) accountable; (*n.*) accountant.

contado, cash.

contador, accountant, teller.

— **ayudante,** junior accountant.

— **de costos,** cost accountant.

— **en jefe,** chief accountant, head teller.

— **fiscal,** government accountant.

— **público titulado,** certified public accountant.

contar, to count.

contingencia, contingency, risk.

contra reembolso, against payment.

contrabando, smuggling.

contracción, contraction.

contrademanda, counter-claim.

contralor de gastos, comptroller.

contraloría, auditor's office.

contramedida, countermeasure.

contraoferta, counteroffer, counterproposal.

contraparte, counterpart.

contrapartida, balancing entry, readjusting entry, contra-entry.

contrarrestar, to counteract.

contratación, transaction.

— **de personal,** employment, hiring.

contratante, contracting party.

contratar, to make a contract.

contratista, contractor.

contrato, contract.

— **a precio alzado,** lump-sum contract.

— **a precio determinado,** fixed-price contract.

—, **bajo,** under contract.

— **colectivo,** collective contract, collective bargaining, labor agreement.

— **de arrendamiento,** lease.

— **de asociación,** articles of partnership.

— **de compraventa,** contract of sale.

— **de empleo,** employment contract, contract of hire.

— **de fletamento,** contract of affreightment.

— **de sociedad,** partnership contract, incorporation papers.

— **implícito,** implied agreement.

— **marítimo,** maritime contract.

— **por administración (costo más honorarios),** cost-plus contract.

contratos de venta en firme, contracts of sale.

contribución, tax, quota.

— **fiscal,** federal tax.

— **inmobiliaria,** real-estate tax.

— **sobre ingreso,** income tax.

contribuyente, taxpayer.

— **evasor,** one who evades taxes.

— **moroso,** delinquent taxpayer.

control, control.

— **de cambios,** exchange control.

— **de existencias,** inventory control.

— **económico comprensivo,** comprehensive economic control.

controlar, to control.

— **la inflación,** to curb inflation.

convenio, agreement, contract.

conversión, conversion.

convertibilidad, convertibility.

convocar, to call, to summon.

convocatoria, notice of a meeting.

cooperar, to cooperate.

copia, copy, transcript.

coproducto, joint product.

copropiedad, joint ownership.

cordón huelguista, picket line.

corporación, corporation, company.

— **controlada,** controlled company.

— **filial,** subsidiary company.

— **no lucrativa,** nonprofit organization.

corredor, broker, jobber.

— **de acciones,** stockbroker.

— **de apuestas,** bookmaker.

— **de bienes raíces,** real-estate broker, realtor.

—**de bolsa,** stockbroker.

— **de fincas,** realtor, real-estate broker.

correo, mail, post office.

— **aéreo,** air mail.

— **certificado,** registered mail.

— **de entrega inmediata,** special-delivery mail.

— **de primera clase,** first-class mail.

— **ordinario,** regular mail.

corresponsal, correspondent, agent.

corretaje, brokerage.

corriente económica, economic flow.

corte de caja, closing and balancing the cash.

corte representativo, cross section.

cosechar, to harvest.

costas, costs.

costeable, profitable.

costo, cost, price.

—, **curvas de,** cost curves.

— **de contrato,** cost of contract.

— **de factores,** factor cost.

— **de montaje,** assembly cost.

— **de operación,** operation cost.

— **de producción,** operating cost.

— **de reposición,** replacement cost.

— **de sustitución,** replacement cost.

— **de vida,** cost of living.

— **directo,** direct cost.

— **efectivo,** actual cost.

— **en plaza,** market price.

— **estimado,** estimated cost.

—, **función del,** cost function.

— **inicial,** historical cost.

— **marginal,** marginal cost.

— **marginal de los factores,** marginal factor cost.

— **marginal de uso,** marginal user cost.

— **o mercado, el que sea más bajo,** cost or market whichever is lower.

— **por unidad,** unit cost.

— **primo,** prime cost.

— **real,** actual cost.

— **reducido,** low cost, reduced cost.

— **según factura,** invoice cost.

—, **seguro, flete y cambio,** cost, insurance, freight and exchange (C.I.F.E.).

—, **seguro y flete,** cost, insurance and freight (C.I.F.)

— **unitario,** unit cost.

— **variable promedio,** average variable cost.

costos, expenses.

— **conexos,** joint costs.

— **de conservación,** maintenance charges.

— **de embalaje,** packing expense.

— **de expedición,** shipping charges.

— **de operación,** operating expenses.

— **indirectos,** indirect cost.

— **presupuestados,** estimated cost.

—, **teoría de,** theory of comparative costs.

costoso, expensive, high-priced.

costumbre comercial, business practice.

cotejar, to compare.

cotidiano, daily.

cotización, quotation, list of prices.

cotizaciones de apertura, opening prices.

crecimiento económico, economic growth.

crédito, credit.

—, **a,** on credit.

— **a corto plazo,** short-term credit.

— **a largo plazo,** long-term credit.

— **abierto,** open credit.

— **cedido,** assigned claim.

— **congelado,** frozen credit.

— **de emergencia,** stop-gap loan.

— **dudoso,** doubtful credit.

— **en moneda extranjera,** credit in foreign exchange.

— **irrevocable,** irrevocable credit.

— **mercantil,** goodwill, reputation.

crisis económica, business depression.

criterio, judgment, policy.

— **comercial,** business judgment.

— **financiero,** method of financing.

— **impositivo,** system of taxation.

cuadruplicado, quadruplicate.

cuantía, quantity, amount.

cuantitativo, quantitative.

cubicación, volume, cubage.

cubrir, to cover, to pay.

cubrirse, to hedge.

cuenta, account, bill.

—, **a,** on account.

— **abierta,** open account.

— **bancaria,** bank account.

— **controladora,** controlling account.

— **corriente,** current account, open account.

— **de ahorros,** savings account.

— **de balance,** balance account.

— **de cierre,** closing account.

— **de cheques,** current account, checking account.

— **de fabricación,** manufacturing account.

— **de gastos,** expense account.

— **de ingresos,** income account.

— **de pérdidas y ganancias,** profit and loss account.

— **de ventas,** sales account.

— **detallada,** itemized account.

— **deudora,** debit account.

— **en participación,** joint account.

— **entre compañías,** inter-company account.

— **particular,** private account.

cuentahabiente, bank depositor.

cuentas, accounts.

— **congeladas,** frozen accounts.

— **de pasivo,** liability accounts.

— **generales,** general accounts.

— **incobrables,** uncollectible accounts, bad debts.

— **mixtas,** mixed accounts.

— **pendientes,** outstanding accounts.

— **por cobrar,** accounts receivable.

— **por pagar,** accounts payable.

— **varias,** sundry accounts.

cultivos básicos, basic crops.

cumplir con las especificaciones, to meet specifications.

cuota, quota, share, allotment.

— **de exportación,** export quota.

— **de importación,** import quota.

cuotas, dues.

cupón, coupon, subshare.

cupones de acción, fractional shares.

curva, curve.

— **de frecuencia,** frequency curve.

— **de la demanda,** demand curve.

— **de probabilidades,** probability curve.

custodia, custody, safe-keeping.

CH

chelín, shilling.

cheque, check.

— **al portador,** check to bearer.

— **aprobado,** certified check.

— **caducado,** stable check.

— **cancelado,** canceled check.

— **certificado,** certified check.

— **de ventanilla,** counter check.

— **de viajero,** traveler's check.

— **pendientes de pago,** outstanding checks.

— **posfechado,** postdated check.

D

daños, damages.

— **dobles,** double damages.

— **emergentes,** consequential damages.

— **materiales,** property damage.

datos, data, information.

— **básicos,** basic information, bench-mark data.

de la vuelta, brought forward.

debe, debit, charge.

— **y haber,** debit and credit.

deber, (*v.*) to owe; (*n.*) obligation.

debitar, to debit.

débito, debit, charge.

decalitro (dal), decaliter (2.642 liquid gal).

decámetro (dam), decameter (32.808 ft).

decenio, ten years.

decifrar, to decode.

decigramo (dg), decigram (1.5432 grains (avdp.)).

decilitro (dl), deciliter (3.3815 fl. oz.).

decímetro (dm), decimeter (3.937 in).

décimo, one-tenth.

declaración, statement.

— **aduanal,** bill of entry.

— **de exportación,** export declaration.

— **(de impuestos) falsa,** false return.

— **fiscal,** income-tax report.

declarar, to declare.

— **una huelga,** to call a strike.

decomisar, to confiscate.

decretar, to decree.

deducción, deduction.

deducible, deductible.

deducir, to deduct.

defectuoso, defective.

deficiencia, deficiency.

déficit, deficit, shortage.

— **de dólares,** dollar gap, dollar shortage.

deflación, deflation.

deflacionado, deflated.

demanda, demand, petition.

—, **comprensión de la,** compression demand.

— **de empleo,** demand for labor.

— **de trabajo,** demand for labor.

— **efectiva,** effective demand.

— **floja,** sluggish demand.

demandado, defendant.

demandante, plaintiff.

demandar, to demand, to claim.

demografía, demography.

— **matemática,** mathematical demography.

— **social,** social demography.

— **teórica,** theoretical demography.

demora, delay.

densidad potencial, potential density.

denunciar, to report, to file a claim.

departamento, department.

— **de archivo,** file department.

— **de compras,** purchasing department.

— **de servicio,** service department.

— **de ventas,** sales department.

depositante, depositor.

depositar, to deposit.

depositario, trustee, bailee, depository.

depósito, deposit.

— **derivado,** derivative deposit.

—, **en,** on deposit.

depósitos en bancos, bank deposits.

depreciación, depreciation.

— **acelerada,** accelerated depreciation.

— **acumulada,** accrued depreciation.

— **combinada,** composite depreciation.

— **contable,** accounting depreciation.

—, **costo de,** depreciation cost.

— **de la moneda,** depreciation of currency.

— **física,** physical depreciation.

— **real,** actual depreciation.

depreciar, to depreciate, to devalue.

depresión, business depression, recession.

derecho, right.

— **comercial,** commercial law.

— **de autor,** copyright.

— **de conversión,** conversion option.

— **de gentes,** international law.

— **de huelga,** right to strike.

— **de patente,** patent rights.

— **de subscripción,** application rights.

— **mercantil,** business law.

— **obrero,** labor laws.

derechos, taxes, duties, rights.

— **adquiridos,** vested rights.

— **de aduana,** custom-house duties.

— **de autor,** copyright.

— **de exportación,** export duties.

— **de importación,** import duties.

— **de propiedad,** property rights.

— **de puerto,** harbor dues.

— **de registro,** registration fees.

— **exclusivos,** exclusive rights.

—, **exento de,** duty-free.

— **portuarios,** port duties.

— **precautorios,** preventive rights.

— **primarios,** primary rights.

— **proteccionistas,** protective duties.

derogar, to revoke.

desautorizado, unauthorized.

descargar, to unload, to discharge.

descartar, discard.

descompensado, unbalanced.

desconfianza, distrust.

descongelar, to unfreeze.

descontable, discountable, bankable.

descontar, to deduct, to discount.

descontinuar, to discontinue.

descubierto, en, overdrawn.

descuento, discount, rebate.

— **bancario,** bank discount.

— **básico,** basic rebate.

—, **factor de,** discount factor.

— **por pronto pago,** cash discount.

—, **tipo de,** discount rate.

desembarcar, to unload.

desembolsar, to disburse.

desempleo, unemployment.

— **cíclico,** cyclical unemployment.

— **estacional,** seasonal unemployment.

desequilibrio de la balanza de pagos, external imbalance.

desfalco, embezzlement, defalcation.

desfavorable, unfavorable.

desinflar, to deflate.

desinterés, lack of interest.

desinversión, disinvestment.

desistirse de la demanda, to abandon a suit.

desleal, unfair.

desobedecer, to disobey.

desocupación, unemployment, idleness.

— **debida a resistencias,** frictional unemployment.

— **involuntaria,** involuntary unemployment.

despacho, office, shipment, message.

desperdicio, scrap, waste.

despido temporal de obreros, lay off.

desplome de precios, collapse of prices.

despoblado, unpopulated.

despojo, plunder, dispossession.

destajo, piecework.

destinatario, consignee.

desuso, obsolescence, disuse.

desutilidad, disutility.

— creciente, increasing disutility.

— marginal, marginal disutility.

detallar, to itemize.

detalle, detail, retail.

detallista, retailer.

detener la inflación, to check inflation.

deterioro, deterioration, damage, wear and tear.

determinismo económico, economic determinism.

deuda, debt.

— a corto plazo, short-term debt.

— consolidada, funded debt, fixed debt.

— exterior, foreign debt.

— flotante, floating debt.

— incobrable, bad debt.

— interior, domestic debt.

— nacional, national debt.

— privilegiada, preferred debt.

deudas de sociedades anónimas, corporate debts.

deudor, debtor.

— moroso, delinquent debtor.

devaluación, devaluation.

devengado, earned, accrued.

devolución, refund.

devoluciones y bonificaciones, returns and allowances.

devolver, to return, to refund.

diagramar, to diagram, to make a graph.

diario, journal, book of original entry.

— de caja, cashbook.

— de compras, purchases journal.

— de ventas, sales journal.

días de gracia, days of grace.

dictamen, report, affidavit.

— de auditoría, auditor's certificate.

diferido, deferred.

dilación, delay.

dimisión, resignation.

dinámico, non-static.

dinero, money.

— caro, dear money.

— mercancía, money-commodity.

dirección cablegráfica, cable address.

directiva, board of directors.

director, director, manager.

dirigente, manager.

discontinuar, to discontinue.

discrepancia, discrepancy, disagreement.

discutir, to discuss.

disidentes, dissenting.

disminuir, to decrease.

disolver, to dissolve.

dispersión, scatter.

—, coeficiente de, scatter coefficient.

—, gráfica de, scatter chart.

disponibilidad, availability, liquidity.

—, en, on hand.

disponible, available, on hand.

distribución, distribution, allotment, breakdown.

diversos, miscellaneous, sundries.

dividendo, dividend.

— de liquidación, liquidating dividend.

— decretado, declared dividend.

— diferido, deferred dividend

— en especie, dividend in kind.

— no reclamado, unclaimed dividend.

— ocasional, irregular dividend.

— omitido, passed dividend.

— parcial, interim dividend.

— preferente, preferred dividend.

dividendos, dividends.

— en acciones, stock dividends.

— en efectivo, cash dividends.

— omitidos, passed dividends.

— por cobrar, dividends receivables.

— por pagar, dividends payable.

divisas, foreign exchange.

— de valor estable, hard currency.

división, division, distribution, department.

doble, double.

—, indemnización, double damages.

—, partida, double entry.

—, patrón, double standard.

— responsabilidad, double liability.

— tributación, double taxation.

documentos, documents.

— contra aceptación, documents against acceptance.

— de embarque, shipping documents.

— por cobrar, notes receivable.

— por pagar, notes payable.

dolo, fraud.

doméstico, domestic, national.

domicilio, address.

dominio, ownership, control.

— **eminente,** eminent domain.
donador, donor.
donar, to donate.
dotar, to endow.
dote, endowment.
dueño, owner.
duopolio, duopoly.
duplicado, duplicate.

duplo, double.
duración
— **media de vida,** life expectancy.
— **probable de vida al nacer,** probable duration of life at birth.
duradero, durable.

E

economía, economy, economics.
— **cerrada,** closed economy.
— **clásica,** classical economics.
— **de abundancia,** economy of abundance.
— **de escasez,** economy of scarcity.
— **de mano de obra,** laborsaving.
— **de monocultivo,** one-crop economy.
— **de tiempo,** timesaving.
— **deficitaria,** deficit economy.
— **dirigida,** centrally planned economy, directed economy.
— **doméstica,** home economics.
— **no monetaria,** noncash economy.
— **planificada,** planned economy.
económica, economic.

—, **corriente,** economic flow.
—, **estructura,** economic pattern.
—, **guerra,** economic warfare.
—, **planeación,** economic planning.
—, **política,** economic policy.
económico, economic.
—, **crecimiento,** economic growth.
—, **determinismo,** economic determinism.
economista, economist.
economizar, to economize, to save.
edad, age.
— **de jubilación,** retirement age.
—, **mayor de,** of age.
— **media al morir,** mean age at death.
—, **menor de,** minor.
—, **redondeada,** rounded age.

efecto inflacionista, inflationary effect.

efectuar el pago, to effect payment.

eficacia marginal del capital, marginal efficiency of capital.

ejecutivo, executive.

—, comité, executive committee.

ejercicio, business year, accounting period.

— anual, calendar year.

—, fin del, end of period.

— fiscal, fiscal year.

elaboración, process.

—, error de, processing error.

—, impuesto por, processing tax.

elevar, to raise, to increase.

— al máximo, to maximize.

embalaje, packing, packing charge.

— para exportación, export packing.

embarcado de menos, short-shipped.

embarcar, to load, to ship.

embargo, embargo.

— precautorio, lien.

embarque, shipment.

emisión, issue.

— excesiva, overissue.

emolumento, salary, fee.

empacar, to pack.

empaque, packing.

empeñar, to pawn.

empeorar, to impair.

emplazamiento de huelga, strike call.

empleado, employee, clerk.

empleados públicos, government employees.

emplear, to employ, to hire.

empleo, employment, job.

— reducido, part-time employment.

— total, full employment.

empleos sucesivos, entre, between jobs.

empresa, enterprise, company.

— clasificada, rated concern.

— estatal, government enterprise.

empréstito, loan.

— de amortización, amortization loan, sinking-fund loan.

— de guerra, war loan.

— exterior, foreign loan.

— interior, domestic loan.

en especie, in kind.

en proceso, work in process.

en serie, assembly-line.

enajenación, abalienation.

enajenar, to alienate.

encarecer, to raise the price.

endosar, to endorse.

endoso, endorsement.

— anterior, previous endorsement.

33

— **calificado,** qualified endorsement.

— **condicional,** conditional endorsement.

— **en blanco,** blank endorsement.

enfermedad profesional, occupational disease.

enganche, down payment, deposit.

engañar, to defraud.

engaño, fraud.

engañoso, misleading.

enjuiciar, to bring suit.

enmienda, amendment.

enriquecerse, to get rich.

ensayo, assay.

entendimiento, understanding, agreement.

entidad, entity.

entrada, entrance.

— **en el debe,** debit entry.

entradas, receipts

— **a caja,** cash receipts.

— **brutas,** gross income, revenue.

— **de cierre,** closing entries.

— **y salidas,** receipts and expenditures.

entre empleos sucesivos, between-jobs.

entrega, delivery.

— **contra reembolso,** cash on delivery.

— **futura,** future delivery.

— **inmediata,** special delivery (letter), spot delivery (of goods).

entregado al costado del vapor, delivered alongside.

envasar, to can, to pack.

envase, container, packing.

enviar fondos, to remit funds.

envío contra reembolso, C.O.D. shipment.

equilibrio, equilibrium.

— **del comercio exterior,** balance of trade.

—**, nivel de,** equilibrium level.

—**, valor de,** equilibrium value.

equipo, equipment.

equitativo, equitable.

erario, public treasury.

erogación, expenditure.

— **capitalizable,** capital expenditure.

error, error, mistake.

— **compensador,** counter-error.

— **constante,** systematic error.

— **cuadrático medio,** mean-square error.

— **de cálculo,** miscalculation.

— **de muestreo,** sampling error.

— **de primera especie,** error of first kind.

— **del muestreo aleatorio,** random sampling error.

— **en encuestas,** error in surveys.

— **medio,** mean error.

— **prescrito,** prescribed error.

— **probable,** probable error.

—**, zona de,** error band.

errores compensados, compensating errors.

escala, scale.

— **de liquidez,** scale of liquidity.

— **de progresión,** scale of progression.

— **de progresión global,** scale of global progression.

— **de repartición,** scale of apportionment.

— **de sueldos,** scale of wages.

— **de valores,** range of values.

— **móvil,** sliding scale.

escalafón de antigüedad, seniority list.

escasa demanda, little demand.

escasa ganancia, small profit.

escasez, scarcity, shortage.

— **de capitales,** scarcity of capital.

— **de crédito,** credit squeeze.

— **de viviendas,** housing shortage.

escaso, scarce.

escrito, por, in writing.

escritura, legal instrument, contract.

— **constitutiva,** corporation charter, incorporation papers.

— **constitutiva y estatutos,** constitution and bylaws.

— **de asociación,** articles of partnership.

— **de compraventa,** bill of sale.

— **de hipoteca,** mortgage deed.

— **de sociedad,** incorporation papers.

— **de venta,** bill of sale.

escrutinio, counting of votes.

escuela comercial, business school.

esfera, sphere, area.

— **de actividad,** field of activity.

— **esterlina,** sterling area.

esforzarse, to endeavor.

esfuerzo, endeavor.

espacio parámetro, parameter space.

especificaciones de embalaje, packing list.

especulador, speculator, dealer.

especular, to especulate.

especulativo, speculative, for profit.

espiral de costos y precios, cost-price spiral.

esqueleto, blank.

esquema, plan, diagram.

esquematizar, to outline.

estabilidad, stability.

— **de precios,** price steadiness.

estabilización, stabilization, equalization.

— **de precios,** price strengthening.

estable, stable.

estación, season.

estacional, seasonal.

estadística, statistics.

estadísticas vitales (demográficas), vital statistics.

estadístico, statistical.

estado, condition, status.

— **anual,** annual report.

— **comparativo,** comparative statement.

— **de cuenta,** statement of account, bank statement.

— **de ingresos,** statement of income.

— **de liquidación,** liquidation statement.

— **de operación,** operating statement.

— **de pérdidas y ganancias,** profit and loss statement.

— **de situación,** statement of condition.

— **en proforma,** pro-forma statement.

— **financiero,** financial statement.

estafa, fraud.

estafar, to defraud.

estancamiento, stagnation.

estándar de vida, standard of living.

estatutario, statutory.

estatuto de limitaciones, statute of limitations.

estatutos, articles of association, bylaws.

estenografía, shorthand.

esterlina, sterling.

estibador, longshoreman.

estimación, estimate, appraisal.

— **lineal,** lineal estimation.

estimador, estimator.

— **de eficiencia máxima,** most-efficient estimator.

— **del máximo de verosimilitud,** maximum likelihood estimator.

estimativo, estimated.

estímulo, inventive.

estipulaciones en política impositiva, canons of taxation.

estratificación geográfica, geographic stratification.

estratos, strata.

estructura económica, economic pattern.

estudio de orientación, pilot study.

evadir impuestos, to evade taxes.

evaluar, to appraise, to evaluate.

evasión, evasion.

— **de capitales,** flight of capital.

— **de impuestos,** tax evasion, tax dodging.

— **fiscal,** tax evasion.

evolución desfavorable, worsening.

ex muelle, ex dock.

excedente, excess, surplus.

— **de capital,** capital surplus.

— **de peso,** overweight.

— **de utilidades,** excess profit.

excedentes agrícolas, surplus crops.

excesivo, excessive.

exceso, excess, surplus.

— **de producción,** glut.

exclusivo, exclusive.

exención, exemption.

— **de impuestos,** tax exemption.

exento, exempt, free.

— **de derechos,** duty-free.

existencia, en, on hand, in stock.

— **inicial,** beginning inventory.

— **mínima,** basic stock.

existencias, stock.

—, **movimiento de,** inventory turnover.

expansión, expansion.

— **crediticia,** credit expansion.

— **vertical,** vertical expansion.

expedidor, shipper, forwarder.

expediente, file, record.

expeditar, to expedite, to facilitate.

experto, expert.

exportación, export.

—, **cuota de,** export quota.

—, **declaración de,** export declaration.

—, **derechos de,** export duty.

—, **gerente de,** export manager.

—, **precio de,** export price.

—, **subsidios para la,** export subsidies.

exportaciones clave, key exports.

exportador, exporter.

exportar, to export.

exposición, display, exposition, fair.

exprés, express.

expropiar, to expropriate.

extracto de cuenta, statement of account.

extranjero, foreigner, alien.

extraoficial, unofficial.

F

fábrica, factory, mill, plant.

fabricación, manufacture.

— **en proceso,** goods in process.

— en serie, mass production.
fabricante, manufacturer.
fabricar, to manufacture.
facilidades, facilities.
— de pago, easy terms of payment.
factible, workable, feasible.
factor, factor.
— de aumento, raising factor.
— de compensación, balancing factor.
— de descuento, discount factor.
— de producción, output factor.
— de tolerancia, tolerance factor.
— para rectificar, calibrating factor.
— real de la demanda, effective depreciation factor.
— real de la depreciación, effective depreciation factor.
factores, factors.
— compensatorios, offsetting factors.
— de producción, production factors.
factura, bill, invoice.
— comercial, commercial invoice.
— consular, consular invoice.
— de venta, bill of sale.
— definitiva, final invoice.
facturar, to bill, to invoice.
falsificación, forgery.

falsificar, to forge.
falso, false.
falta, fault, deficiency, lack.
— de demanda, sales resistance.
— de pago, nonpayment.
— de peso, short weight.
falto de existencia, out of stock.
familia de tamaño medio, medium-size family.
fanega, bushel.
fase descendente, downswing.
favorable, favorable, advantageous.
fecha, date.
— de entrega, date of delivery.
— de vencimiento, maturity date, due date.
— media de vencimiento, equated date.
feria, fair, market.
fiador, bondsman, surety, backer.
fianza, bond, bail.
— de averías, average bond.
— hipotecaria, mortgage.
fiar, to give credit.
fichero, file.
fideicomiso, trust.
— pasivo, passive trust, dry trust.
fiduciario, fiduciary.
fijo, fixed.
filial, branch, subsidiary.

financiamiento, financing.

— compensatorio, compensatory financing.

— deficitario, deficit financing.

financiar, to finance.

financiero, financial.

finanzas, finance.

finiquitar, to settle and close an account.

finiquito, full settlement.

firma, firm, signature.

— autorizada, authorized signature.

— comercial, commercial house.

— en blanco, blank signature.

firmante, signer.

firmar, to sign.

— mancomunadamente, to sign jointly.

fiscal, auditor, controller, district attorney, fiscal.

—, año, fiscal year.

fisco, national treasury.

físico, physical.

fletar, to charter.

flete, freight, freight rate.

— aéreo, air freight.

— falso, dead freight.

— marítimo, ocean freight.

— pagable a destino, freight collect.

— pagado, freight prepaid.

— por carro entero, carload rate.

— por cobrar, freight collect.

flotante, floating.

fluctuaciones, fluctuations.

— cíclicas, cyclical fluctuations.

— del mercado, market fluctuations.

foja, folio.

folio, folio, page.

fondo, fund.

— de amortización, sinking fund.

— de caja chica, petty cash fund.

— de contingencia, contingent fund.

— de depreciación, depreciation fund.

— de estabilización, equalization fund.

— de expansión, development fund.

— de huelga, strike fund.

— de pensión, pension fund.

— de pensiones de vejez, superannuation fund.

— de reserva, reserve fund.

— de seguro propio, insurance fund.

— en fideicomiso, trust fund.

— fijo de caja, cash imprest.

— mutualista, mutual fund.

— para accidentes industriales, industrial insurance fund.

— **para imprevistos,** contingency fund.

— **renovable,** revolving fund.

— **revolvente,** rotary fund.

fondos, funds.

— **disponibles,** ready cash, cash and bank deposits.

— **en efectivo,** cash funds, monies.

— **insuficientes,** no funds, insufficient funds.

— **públicos,** government bonds.

forma de pago, terms of payment.

fraccionamiento, subdivision, development.

— **de acciones,** share split.

fraccionar, to subdivide.

franco, free, exempt.

— **a bordo,** free on board (F.O.B.)

— **de derechos,** duty-free.

— **de porte,** postage-free.

— **en el muelle,** free on dock.

— **en fábrica,** ex factory, ex mill.

franqueo, postage.

franquicia, exemption, franchise.

fraude, fraud.

frugalidad forzada, forced frugality.

fuerza, force.

— **de trabajo,** working force.

— **mayor,** force majeure, act of God.

fulana de tal, Mary Doe.

fulano de tal, John Doe.

función, function, operation.

— **característica operante,** operating characteristic function.

— **consumo,** consumption function.

— **de densidad,** density function.

— **de ponderación,** weight function.

— **del riesgo,** risk function.

— **demanda,** demand function.

funcionario, official.

fundación, endowment.

fundo, land property.

furgón, freight car, boxcar.

fusión, merger.

futuros, futures.

—, **mercado de,** futures market.

G

galón, gallon (3.785 l.)

ganancia, profit.

— **bruta,** gross profit.

ganancias, gains, profits.

— **de capital,** capital gains.

— **por hora,** hourly earnings.

— **previstas,** anticipated profits.

— **y pérdidas,** profit and loss.

ganar, to earn, to gain.

garantía, warranty, security.

— **crediticia,** credit guarantee.

— **hipotecaria,** mortgage.

— **prendaria,** collateral.

garantizar, to guarantee.

gastar, to spend.

gastarse, to wear.

gasto adicional, additional expense.

gastos, expenses, costs.

— **acumulados,** accrued expenses.

— **bancarios,** bank charges.

— **de almacenaje,** storage charges.

— **de capital,** capital charges.

— **de cobranza,** collection expenses.

— **de embarque,** shipping charges.

— **de explotación,** operating expenses.

— **de mantenimiento de la familia,** family living expenditures.

— **de operación,** operating expenses.

— **de publicidad,** advertising expenses.

— **de viaje,** traveling expenses.

— **deficitarios,** deficit spending.

— **familiares,** family expenses.

— **generales,** general expenses.

— **imprevistos,** incidental expenses, incidentals.

— **marginales,** marginal expenditures.

— **menores,** petty expenses.

— **ordinarios de operación,** running expenses.

— **varios,** sundry expenses.

genuino, genuine.

gerencia, management, manager's office.

— **de fabricación,** production department.

— **de ventas,** sales department.

gerente, manager.

— **de exportación,** export manager.

— **de ventas,** sales manager.

girado, drawee.

girador, drawer.

girar, to draw (a draft).

— **en descubierto,** to overdraw.

— **un cheque,** to draw a check.

— **una letra,** to draw a draft.

giro, draft.

— **a la vista,** sight draft.
— **a plazo,** time draft.
— **bancario,** bank draft.
— **postal,** money order.
gobierno, government.
graduar, to graduate, to classify.
gráfica, graph, chart.
gramo (g), gram (15.432 grains (avdp.)).
grano, grain.
gratis, free.

gratuito, free.
gravable, taxable.
gravamen, lien, tax, encumbrance.
— **de factor,** factor's lien.
gravar, to tax.
gremio, labor union.
grupo humano, cohort.
guerra económica, economic warfare.
guía de carga, waybill, cargo receipt.

H

haber, credit.
haberes, wages.
habilidad, skill, proficiency.
hacer, to make, to do.
— **coincidir,** to bring into conformity.
— **cumplir,** to enforce.
— **efectivo,** to cash, to collect.
— **entrega,** to deliver.
— **saber,** to notify.
— **un pedido,** to place an order.
hectárea (ha), hectare (2.471 acres).
hectogramo (hg), hectogram (3.5274 ounces (avdp.)).
hectolitro (hl), hectoliter (26.4178 liquid gal.).
hectómetro (hm), hectometer (328.083 ft).
herramientas, tools.

hipoteca, mortgage.
— **colectiva,** general mortgage.
—, **primera,** first mortgage.
hipótesis compuesta, composite hypothesis.
hoja, sheet.
— **de balance,** balance sheet.
— **de trabajo,** work sheet.
honorarios, fees.
honrado, honest.
hora, hour, time.
— **mano de obra,** man-hours.
— **oficial,** standard time.
hora-máquina, machine-hour.
horario, timetable.
horas laborables, working hours.
huelga, strike.

42

— **de brazos caídos,** sit-down strike.

— **de solidaridad,** sympathetic strike.

— **loca,** wildcat strike.

huelguista, striker.

huída de capitales, flight of capital.

I

idear, to devise.

identificación, identification.

igual remuneración por igual trabajo, equal pay for equal work.

igualar, to equalize, to equate.

igualdad, equality, uniformity.

ilegal, illegal.

iliquidez, illiquidity.

impagable, unpayable.

imponer impuestos, to levy taxes.

importador, importer.

importar, to import.

importe, amount, price.

— **a pagar,** amount due.

— **bruto,** gross amount.

— **global,** lump sum.

— **marginal de ventas,** marginal proceeds.

— **neto,** net amount.

imposición, tax, taxation.

— **de capitales,** investment of capital.

— **de la renta,** income tax.

— **degresiva,** degressive taxation.

— **fiscal,** federal tax.

impracticable, unfeasible.

imprevistos, contingencies.

imprimir dinero, to print money.

improductivo, unproductive.

improvisado, makeshift.

impuesto, tax, duty, levy.

— **a la exportación,** export duty.

— **adicional,** surtax.

— **aduanal,** customs duties.

— **causado,** tax incurred.

— **compensatorio,** compensatory duty.

— **de guerra,** war tax.

— **estatal,** state tax.

— **fiscal,** internal revenue tax.

— **no pagado a tiempo,** delinquent tax.

— **personal,** personal tax.

— **por persona,** poll tax.

— **predial,** property tax, land tax.

— **sobre compraventa,** sales tax.

— **sobre donaciones,** gift tax.

— **sobre herencias,** inheritance tax.

— **sobre ingresos mercantiles,** gross-income tax.

— **sobre utilidades,** profit tax.

— **sobre ventas,** excise tax.

— **único,** single tax.

impuestos

— **acumulados,** accrued taxes.

— **atrasados,** back taxes.

— **de represalia,** retaliatory tariff.

impulso aleatorio, random impulse process.

inaceptable, unacceptable.

inacumulable, noncumulative.

inadecuado, inadequate.

inalienable, inalienable.

inamovible, nonremovable.

incapacidad, disability.

— **absoluta permanente,** permanent total disability.

— **parcial permanente,** permanent partial disability.

incapacitado, disabled, disqualified.

incautación, seizure.

incentivo, incentive.

— **para invertir,** inducement to invest.

incidencia, incidence.

inciso, paragraph.

incluyendo impuestos indirectos, inclusive of indirect taxes.

incobrable, uncollectible.

inconvertible, inconvertible.

incorporación, incorporation

incorporar, to incorporate. to merge.

incrementar, to increase.

indemnización, indemnity, compensation.

— **por despido,** dismissal wage, terminal wage.

indicador de cotizaciones, stock ticker.

indicador financiero, financial index, stock market averages.

índice, index, ratio.

— **cruzado,** cross reference.

— **de costo unitario,** index of unit cost.

— **de crédito,** credit rating.

— **de la producción física,** index of physical production.

— **de libros,** accountant's index.

— **de liquidez,** liquidity ratio.

— **de mortalidad,** death rate.

— **de mortalidad comparativa,** index of comparative mortality.

— **de ocupación,** employment index number.

— **de precios,** price index.

— **de precios de mercancías de consumo,** consumer's price index.

— **de precios de mercaderías,** commodity price index.

— **de producción,** production index.

— **de valores unitarios,** unit value index.

— **de ventas,** sales ratio.

— **no ponderado,** unweighted index.

— **ponderado,** weighted index.

industria, industry.

— **naciente,** infant industry.

industrias, industries.

— **clave,** key industries.

ineficaz, ineffectual.

ineficiencia, inefficiency.

inelástico, inelastic.

inestabilidad, instability.

inestable, unstable.

inexacto, incorrect, inaccurate.

inexperto, unskilled.

inflación, inflation.

— **del crédito,** credit inflation.

— **lenta,** creeping inflation.

inflacionario, inflationary.

inflado, inflated.

influencia depresiva, depressing influence.

informar, to report.

informe, report, information.

— **de auditoría,** audit report.

— **de crédito,** credit report.

— **largo o detallado,** long-form report.

infracción, infringement.

infrascrito, undersigned.

ingreso, income.

— **de los factores de producción,** factor income.

— **del trabajo,** labor income.

— **familiar,** family income.

— **gravable,** taxable income.

— **libre de impuestos,** tax-free income.

— **medio,** average earnings.

— **neto,** net income.

— **ordinario,** current revenue.

— **real,** real income.

ingresos, earnings.

— **adicionales,** additional income.

— **brutos,** gross receipts, gross earnings.

— **acumulados,** accrued income.

—, **declaración de,** income statement.

— **totales,** total receipts.

— **y gastos,** income and expenditures.

injusto, unfair, inequitable.

inmigración, immigration.

inmuebles, real estate.

inquilino, tenant, lessee.

inscribir, to register, to inscribe, to enroll.

inscribirse, to enroll.

insoluto, unpaid.

insolvencia, insolvency, bankruptcy.

inspeccionar, to inspect.

inspector fiscal, tax examiner.

instalaciones, facilities.
instructivo, instruction sheet.
— de contabilidad, plan of accounts.
instrumento, instrument.
instrumentos negociables, commercial paper, negotiable instruments.
insumo, input, investment, expenditure.
— corriente, current input.
— producto, input–output.
intangibles, intangibles.
integrante, built-in.
íntegro, integral, complete.
intensidad, intensity.
intercambio, interchange.
interés, interest.
— acumulado, accrued interest.
— compuesto, compound interest.
— corriente, current interest.
— legal, interest at legal rate.
— mayoritario, majority interest.
— minoritario, minority interest.
— simple, simple interest.
— que se acumula, accruing interest.
interés-dividendo, interest-dividend.
intereses creados, vested interest.

intereses vencidos, interest due.
interestatal, interstate.
intermediario, middleman, jobber.
intérprete, interpreter.
intervalo, interval.
— de agrupamiento, grouping interval.
interventor, auditor.
intransferible, not transferable.
inútil, useless.
invalidez, disability, invalidity.
inventariar, to take stock.
inventario, inventory.
— final o de cierre, closing inventory.
— físico, physical inventory.
— inicial, opening inventory.
— por unidades, unit inventory.
— valorado, valued inventory.
inversión, investment, expenditure.
— básica, basic investment.
— bruta, gross investment.
— en especie, investment in kind.
— excesiva, overinvestment.
—, multiplicador de, investment multiplier.
—, política de, investment policy.
inversionista, investor.

invertir, to invest.
investigación, research.

irredimible, not redeemable.
irrevocable, irrevocable.

J

jefe, head, boss, manager, chief.
— **de personal,** personnel manager.
— **de producción,** production manager.
jornada, day's work.
— **doble,** double shift.
— **reducida,** part-time employment.
jornadas-obrero, man-days.
jornalero, laborer.
jubilación, retirement.
—, **edad de,** retirement age.

jubilar, to pension, to retire.
juego de bolsa, stock speculation.
juicio, judgment, lawsuit, trial.
junta, committee, board, meeting.
— **de conciliación,** conciliation board.
— **de directores,** board of directors.
— **del consejo,** board meeting.
jurado, jury.
justo, correct, fair.

K

kilogramo (kg), kilogram (2.205 pounds (avdp.)).
kilolitro (kl), kiloliter

(264.178 liquid gal).
kilómetro (km), kilometer (0.621 mile).

L

labor productiva, productive labor.
lado deudor, debit side.
lanzar al mercado, to put on sale.

latifundio, large estate.
legal, legal.
legalizar, to legalize.
legislación, legislation.
legítimo, legitimate, genuine.

47

leonino, unfair, one-sided.
letra, draft, bill.
— **a la vista,** sight draft.
— **bancaria,** bank draft.
— **de cambio,** bill of exchange.
— **protestada,** protested bill.
letras, bills.
— **a cobrar,** bills receivable.
— **a pagar,** bills payable.
levantar la sesión, to adjourn the meeting.
ley, law, statute.
— **de la oferta y la demanda,** law of supply and demand.
— **de los promedios,** law of averages.
— **de rendimientos crecientes,** law of increasing returns.
— **de sociedades,** corporation law.
— **del trabajo,** labor code.
— **fiscal,** tax law.
— **mercantil,** commercial code.
leyes, laws.
— **laborales,** labor laws.
— **suntuarias,** sumptuary laws.
libertad, liberty, right.
— **de comercio,** free trade.
— **de empresa,** free enterprise.
libra (lb), pound.

— **esterlina,** pound sterling.
librado, drawee.
librador, drawer.
libre, free, exempt.
— **a bordo,** free on board.
— **al costado del vapor,** free alongside.
— **cambio,** free trade, free rate of exchange.
— **comercio,** free trade.
— **competencia,** free competition.
— **de cargos,** free of charges.
— **de derechos,** duty-free.
— **de gastos,** free of charges.
— **de gravamen,** free and clear.
— **de impuesto,** tax-free, tax-exempt.
— **de porte,** postage-free.
— **elección,** free choice.
libreta de cheques, check book.
libro, book.
— **borrador,** daybook.
— **de actas,** minute book.
— **de caja,** cashbook.
— **de caja chica,** petty cash book.
— **de compras,** purchases journal.
— **de cuentas,** account book, ledger.
— **de cheques,** checkbook.
— **de existencias,** stock book.

— **de facturas,** invoice register

— **de pedidos,** order book.

— **de primera entrada,** book
of original entry.

— **de ventas,** sales journal.

— **diario,** journal.

— **mayor,** ledger.

— **mayor general,** general
ledger.

libros auxiliares, subsidiary
books.

licencia, license, permit.

— **de cambio,** exchange permit.

— **de exportación,** export permit.

— **de importación,** import
permit.

—, **derechos de,** license
fees.

— **de patente,** patent license.

licenciado, lawyer, licensed,
having a degree.

— **en economía,** economist.

licitación, bidding.

licitar, to bid.

lícito, legal.

limitado, limited, restricted.

límite, limit.

— **de crédito,** line of credit,
loan ceiling.

— **de precio,** price ceiling.

límites de tolerancia no

paramétricas, nonparametric tolerance limits.

lingote, ingot.

liquidación, settlement.

— **de sociedad,** dissolution of
partnership.

liquidado, liquidated, paid in
full.

liquidar una cuenta, to settle
an account.

liquidez, liquidity.

—, **escala de,** scale of liquidity.

—, **patrón de,** standard of
liquidity.

—, **preferencia por la,** liquidity preference.

—, **prima de,** liquidity premium.

líquido, liquid.

lista, list.

— **de precios,** price list.

— **de raya,** payroll.

litigio, lawsuit.

litro (l), liter (1.057 liquid
quarts).

lote, lot, share.

lucha de clases, class struggle.

lucrativo, lucrative, profitable.

lucro, profit.

— **bruto,** gross profit.

— **líquido,** net profit.

LL

llenar una orden, to fill an order.
llevar, to carry.
— cuentas, to keep accounts.

— en los libros, to carry in the books.
— un registro, to keep a record.

M

malversación, misappropriation, embezzlement.
mancomunadamente, jointly.
mancomunado (a), joint.
—, cuenta, joint account.
manifestación de impuesto, tax return.
manifiesto, manifest.
maniobras de bolsa, stock speculation.
manipulación de precios, rigging of prices.
mano de obra, manpower.
— disponible, available labor.
mantenimiento, maintenance.
manufactura, manufacture.
— en proceso, work in process.
manufacturar, to manufacture, to process.
mapa, map, chart.
máquina, machine.
— de escribir, typewriter.

— registradora, cash register.
maquinaria y equipo, machinery and equipment.
marca, brand.
— de fábrica, trademark.
— registrada, trademark.
margen, margin
— de preferencia, margin of preference.
— de seguridad, margin of safety.
— de utilidades, margin of profits.
— del dumping, margin of dumping.
marginal, marginal.
materia prima, raw material.
mayor, wholesale.
—, al por, at wholesale.
— de edad, of age.
—, libro, ledger.
mayoreo, wholesale.
mayoría de votos abrumadora, landslide.

mayorista, wholesaler.
mecanización, mechanization.
mecanógrafa, typist.
mecanografía, typewriting.
media aritmética ponderada, weighted arithmetic mean.
media geométrica ponderada, weighted geometric mean.
media ponderada, weighted mean.
medida, measure, size.
medidas contrainflacionistas, counterinflationary measures.
medio ponderado, weighted average.
medios de comunicación, means of communication.
medir, to measure.
mejor postor, highest bidder.
mejorar, to improve.
mejoras, improvements.
memoria de quiebra, act of bankruptcy.
menor de edad, minor.
mensaje, message.
— nocturno, night message.
— ordinario, ordinary message.
— urgente, urgent message.
mensual, monthly.
mensualidad, monthly payment.

menudeo, retail.
mercader, merchant.
mercaderías, goods.
mercado, market.
— abierto, open market.
— alcista, bull market.
— bajista, bear market.
— bursátil de acciones, stock market.
—, contracción del, business contraction.
— de cambios, exchange market.
— de futuros, futures market.
— del comprador, buyer's market.
— flojo, dull market, sagging market.
— libre, open market, free market.
— negro, black market.
—, tendencia del, business trend.
mercadotecnia, marketing.
mercancía, merchandise.
— compuesta, composite commodity.
mercancías, goods.
— de calidad, quality goods.
— en tránsito, goods in transit.
— pagaderas en dólares, dollar commodities.
— perecederas, perishable goods.

mercantil, commercial, mercantile.

merma, decrease, shrinkage, loss.

mes, month.

metalismo, bullionism.

método, method.

— **de amortización decreciente,** declining balance method.

— **de los componentes,** component method.

— **de los puntos elegidos,** method of selected points.

— **de porcentaje de terminación,** percentage of completion method.

— **de precio de menudeo,** retail method.

— **de probabilidad,** presumptive method.

— **del menudeo,** retail method.

— **del precio de la última compra,** price of last purchase method.

— **del precio del mercado,** market price method.

— **inductivo,** inductive method.

— **libre,** open market.

— **numérico gráfico,** graphical-numerical method.

metro (m), meter (1.094 yards).

— **cuadrado** (m²), square meter (1.196 square yards) (10.764 ft²).

— **cúbico** (m³), cubic meter (1.308 cubic yards).

miembro, member.

— **titular,** regular member.

— **vitalicio,** life member.

migración permanente, permanent migration.

migraciones periódicas, periodic migrations.

milésimo, thousandth.

miligramo (mg), milligram (0.0154 grain (avdp.)).

mililitro (ml), milliliter (0.0338 fl oz).

milímetro (mm), millimeter (0.03937 in.).

milla, mile.

milla cuadrada, square mile.

millar, thousand.

millón, million.

mina, mine.

minería, mining.

minoría, minority.

minutas, minutes (of a meeting).

mitad, half.

mobiliario y equipo, furniture and fixtures.

modelo mixto, mixed model.

moneda, currency.

— **blanda,** soft currency.

— **convertible,** convertible currency, hard currency.

— **de curso legal,** legal tender.

— **de papel,** paper money.

— **de plata,** silver coin.

— **de valor constante,** constant currency.

— **de valor inestable,** soft currency.

— **en circulación,** outstanding money.

— **estable,** sound money, hard currency.

— **extranjera,** foreign currency.

— **falsa,** counterfeit money.

— **manipulada,** managed currency.

monetario, monetary.

—**, salario,** money wage.

monocultivo, monoculture.

monopolio, monopoly, trust.

monopolista, monopolist.

monopolizar, to monopolize.

monto, amount

— **neto,** net amount.

moratorio, moratory.

mordida, graft.

mortalidad, mortality, death rate.

— **prevista,** expected mortality.

— **real,** actual mortality.

motivo, motive.

— **especulativo,** speculative motive.

— **lucro,** profit motive.

— **negocios,** business motive.

— **precaución,** precautionary motive.

— **transacción,** transactions motive.

movilidad del trabajo, mobility of labor.

movimientos, movements.

— **de capital,** capital movements.

— **de natalidad,** movements in birth.

muestra, sample.

— **contrabalanceada,** balanced sample.

— **controlada,** controlled sample.

— **de autocorrección,** self-correcting sample.

— **no aleatoria,** nonrandom sample.

— **piloto,** pilot sample.

— **representativa,** representative sample.

— **sin bias,** unbiased sample.

— **sin valor,** sample without value.

— **sucesiva,** sequential sample.

muestras concordantes, matched samples.

muestreo, sampling.

— **al azar,** random sampling.

—**, bias del,** sample bias.

— **de líneas,** line sampling.

— **de probabilidad,** probability sampling.

—, **espacio de,** sample space.
— **intensivo,** intensive sampling.
—, **línea de,** sample line.
— **mixto,** mixed sampling.
— **proporcional,** proportional sampling.
—, **punto de,** sample point.
— **restringido,** restricted sampling.
— **sistemático,** systematic sampling.
—, **tolerancia del,** sample tolerance.

multa, fine, penalty.
multar, to fine.
multifásico, multiple-phase.
multilateral, multilateral.
múltiple, multiple.
multiplicador, multiplier.
— **constante,** constant multiplier.
— **de inversión,** investment multiplier.
— **finito,** finite multiplier.
multiplicar, to multiply.
múltiplo común, common multiple.

N

nacionalizar, to nationalize.
negativa, refusal.
negligencia, negligence.
negociabilidad, marketability.
negociable, negotiable.
negociar, to trade, to deal, to negotiate.
negocio, business, transaction.
— **al por menor,** retail trade.
— **al por mayor,** wholesale trade.
neto, net.
nivel, level.
— **de equilibrio,** equilibrium level.
— **de precios,** price level.
— **de salarios,** wage level.

— **de significación,** significance level.
— **de vida,** standard of living.
nivelar, to level.
no clasificado, unclassified.
no dividido, undivided.
no entregado, undelivered.
no ganado, unearned.
no gravable, nontaxable.
no renovable, nonrenewable.
no repartido, undistributed.
nombramiento, appointment.
nombrar, to appoint, to designate.
nómina de sueldos, payroll.
nominal, nominal.
normal, standard.

normas contables, accounting standards.

normas de auditoría, auditing standards.

nota, note.

— de cargo, debit note.

— de crédito, credit note.

— de remisión, shipping note.

notaría, notary's office.

notario, notary.

— público, notary public.

notificar, to notify, to advise.

nulificar, to cancel.

nulo, null.

— y sin valor, null and void.

número, number, figure, digit.

— de orden, serial number.

— de serie, serial number.

— entero, whole number.

— muestral promedio, average sample number.

— óptimo, optimum number.

— par, even number.

números redondos, round numbers.

O

obligación, debenture, debt, liability, indebtedness.

— limitada, limited liability.

obligaciones, liabilities, debentures.

— a corto plazo, short-term liabilities.

— a largo plazo, long-term liabilities.

— al portador, bearer paper.

— hipotecarias, mortgage bonds.

— mercantiles, commerical paper.

obligacionista, debenture holder.

obrero, worker, laborer.

— calificado, skilled worker.

obrero-hora, man-hour.

obstáculo, handicap.

ocioso, idle.

ocupación, occupation.

—, baja de la, decreasing employment.

—, multiplicador de, employment multiplier.

— total, full employment.

oferta, bid, offer.

—, elasticidad de la, elasticity of supply.

— en firme, firm offer.

— mejor, best bid.

— sellada, sealed bid.

— y demanda, supply and demand.

oficina, office, agency, bureau.

— **central,** main office.
— **de correos,** post office.
oficinista, office clerk.
oficio, trade, craft.
omisión, omission.
omitir, to omit.
onza (oz), ounce.
— **avoirdupois,** ounce avoirdupois.
— **Troy,** ounce Troy.
opción de compra, option to
purchase.
operar, to run, to operate, to
transact, to act.
operario, workman, worker.

optativo, optional.
orden, order.
— **de compra,** purchase order
— **de entrega,** delivery order.
— **de pago,** payment order.
— **del día,** order of the day.
ordinario, regular.
organizar, to organize, to
constitute.
origen, origin, source.
original, original.
oro, gold.
— **en barras,** bar gold.
otorgar fianza, to put up a
bond.

P

pacto, agreement, deal.
— **de caballeros,** gentlemen's
agreement.
padrón, register, list.
paga, payment, wages.
— **de marcha,** severance pay.
pagadero, payable.
— **a la orden,** payable to order.
— **a la vista,** due to demand.
— **a plazos,** payable in installments.
— **al entregar,** cash on delivery (C.O.D.).
— **al portador,** payable to
bearer.
— **en efectivo,** payable in cash.

pagado, paid.
— **íntegramente,** paid in full.
pagador, paymaster, paying
teller, payer.
pagar, to pay.
— **a cuenta,** to pay on account.
— **en abonos,** to pay by
installments.
— **por completo,** to pay in
full.
pagaré, promissory note,
I.O.U.
— **a la vista,** demand note.
pago, payment.
— **a cuenta,** payment on account, down-payment.

— **adelantado,** advance payment.

—**al contado,** cash payment.

— **contra documentos,** cash against documents.

— **total,** full payment.

pagos, payments.

— **en oro,** gold payments.

— **escalonados,** progress payments.

páguese

— **a la orden de,** pay to the order of.

— **al portador,** pay to the bearer.

país de origen, source country.

papel moneda, paper money.

papeleo, red tape.

papeles, documents, papers.

par, a la, at par.

—**, bajo,** below par.

—**, sobre,** above par.

parcela, parcel of land.

paridad, parity, par.

— **adquisitiva,** parity in purchasing power.

— **cambiaria,** par of exchange.

paro, shutdown, strike, stoppage.

— **general,** general strike.

— **obrero,** strike.

— **patronal,** lockout.

párrafo, paragraph.

partes

— **contratantes,** contracting parties.

— **interesadas,** interested parties.

participación, share, interest.

— **de control,** controlling interest.

— **de utilidades,** profit sharing.

particular, private.

partida, lot, item.

— **de crédito,** credit item.

— **simple,** single entry.

pasaporte, passport.

pasar, to pass.

— **a otra hoja,** to carry forward.

— **al debe,** to debit.

— **la lista,** to call the roll.

pasivo, passive.

— **a largo plazo,** long-term liabilities.

— **acumulado,** accrued liabilities.

— **asumido,** assumed liabilities.

— **comercial,** current liabilities.

— **consolidado,** funded debt.

— **contingente,** contingent liabilities.

— **de capital,** capital liabilities.

— **diferido,** deferred liabilities.

— **directo,** direct liabilities.

— **fijo,** fixed liabilities.

— **flotante,** current liabilities.

— **real,** actual liabilities.

patentado, patented.

patentar, to patent.

patente, patent, license, franchise.

— **en tramitación,** patent pending.

— **primitiva,** basic patent.

patentes y marcas, patent and trademark.

patrimonio, capital, net worth.

patrocinar, to sponsor.

patrón, employer.

— **de liquidez,** standard of liquidity.

— **doble,** double standard, bimetallism.

— **oro,** gold standard.

— **plata,** silver standard.

patronato, board of trustees.

peaje, toll.

peculado, peculation.

pedido, order.

— **de compra,** purchase order.

— **en firme,** firm order.

— **urgente,** rush order.

pendiente, outstanding, pending, in abeyance.

— **de pago,** unpaid.

pensión, annuity.

— **de invalidez,** disability benefit.

— **de retiro,** retirement pension.

— **diferida,** deferred annuity.

— **familiar,** family allowance.

pérdida, loss, waste.

—, **con,** at sacrifice.

— **total,** absolute total loss.

pérdidas y ganancias, estado de, profit-and-loss statement.

perímetro, perimeter.

período, period.

— **de bonanza,** boom.

— **de gracia (para pagar una deuda),** grace period.

perito, expert, appraiser.

permanente, permanent.

—, **incapacidad absoluta,** permanent total disability.

—, **incapacidad parcial,** permanent partial disability.

—, **migración,** permanent migration.

permeado de, permeated with.

permiso, permit, license.

— **de exportación,** export permit.

— **de importación,** import permit.

permuta, barter.

perpetuidad, perpetuity.

perpetuo, perpetual.

personal, personnel, force, private.

— **de oficina,** office force.

— **de ventas,** sales force.

— **eventual,** temporary workers.

— **obrero,** labor force.

pesar, to weigh.

peso, weight.

— **bruto,** gross weight.

— **legal,** legal weight.

— **muerto,** dead weight.

pie, foot.

— **cuadrado,** square foot.

— **cúbico,** cubic foot.

pinta, pint.

plan, plan, scheme, program.

planeación económica, economic planning.

planificación, planning.

plano, plan, drawing, map, chart.

plazo, time, term.

— **de entrega,** time of delivery.

— **fijo,** fixed term.

pliego de peticiones, list of demands.

pluralidad, plurality.

plusvalía, goodwill, increased value.

población, population.

— **abierta,** open population.

— **logística,** logistic population.

—, **movimiento general de la,** general population movement.

— **óptima,** optimum population.

— **susceptible de tomar empleo,** employable population.

pobreza, poverty.

poder, power, strength.

— **adquisitivo,** purchasing power.

— **amplísimo,** full power.

—, **carta,** power of attorney.

— **para gastar,** spending power.

— **para negociar,** bargaining power.

—, **por,** by proxy.

política, policy.

— **anticíclica,** contracyclical policy.

— **arancelaria,** tariff policy.

— **crediticia,** credit policy.

— **de austeridad,** austerity program, policy of restraint.

— **de existencias estabilizadores,** buffer stock plan.

— **de inversión,** investment policy.

— **de puerta abierta,** open-door policy.

— **de restricción de créditos,** tight-money policy.

— **de sostenimiento de precios,** price-support policy.

— **de ventas,** sales policy.

— **económica,** economic policy.

— **hacendaria,** financial policy.

— **impositiva o tributaria,** tax policy.

póliza, policy.

— **a todo riesgo,** all-risk policy.

— **abierta,** blanket policy.

— **colectiva o de grupo,** group policy.

— **de averías,** average policy.

— **de fidelidad,** fidelity bond.

— **de seguro,** insurance policy.

— **del último superviviente,** last-survivor policy.

— **dotal,** endowment policy.

— **limitada,** limited policy.

ponderado, weighted.

—**, promedio,** weighted average.

ponderar, to weight.

por, per.

— **cabeza,** per capita.

— **ciento,** per cent, percentage.

— **cobrar,** receivable.

— **día,** per diem.

— **mayor,** wholesale.

— **menor,** retail.

— **pagar,** payable.

— **persona,** per capita.

— **poder,** by proxy.

porcentaje, percentage.

— **anual de aumento,** annual percent of increase.

— **de utilidades,** percentage of profits.

porciento, percentage.

pormenorizar, to detail, to itemize.

portador, bearer.

—**, al,** to bearer.

portafolio, portfolio.

porte, freight, carriage.

— **de correos,** postage.

posdata, postscript.

poseedor, holder, possessor, owner.

posfechado, postdated.

posición, position.

posponer, to postpone, to extend.

postal, postal.

postor más bajo, low bidder.

postura, bid.

potencia de una prueba, strength of test.

potencialidad económica, economic possibilities.

práctica comercial, commercial usage.

precio, price, worth.

— **al contado,** cash price.

— **al mayoreo,** wholesale price.

— **actual,** market or current price.

— **convenido,** agreed price.

— **de avalúo,** assessed valuation.

— **de competencia,** competitive price.

— **de compra,** buying price, purchase price.

— **de costo,** cost price.

— **de emisión,** issue price.

— **de exportación,** export price.

— **de fábrica,** factory price.

— **de lista,** list price.

— **de menudeo,** retail price.

— **de oferta,** offered price.

— **de paridad,** parity price.

— **de venta,** selling price.

— **del mercado,** market price.

— **dominante,** prevailing price.

— **justo,** fair value.

— **máximo,** top price.

— **medio,** average price.

— **mínimo,** floor price.

— **módico,** moderate price.

— **muy rebajado,** knock-out price.

— **piloto,** price leader.

— **probable,** prospective price.

— **redondo,** all-round price.

— **según contrato,** price as provided in the contract.

— **sostenido,** support price.

— **techo,** ceiling price.

— **tope,** ceiling price.

— **unitario o por unidad,** unit price.

precios

—, **ajuste de,** price adjustment.

— **al cierre,** closing price.

— **al menudeo,** retail prices.

— **bursátiles,** stock-exchange quotations.

—, **caída de,** drop of prices.

— **de apertura,** opening prices.

— **de monopolio,** monopoly prices.

—, **estabilidad de,** price steadiness.

—, **estabilización de,** price strengthening.

—, **hacer bajar los,** to force prices down.

— **mínimos,** floor prices.

— **oficiales,** official prices.

— **oro,** gold prices.

—, **política de sostenimiento de,** price-support policy.

—, **resistencia contra los altos,** price resistance.

—, **subsidio de,** price subsidy.

preferencia por la liquidez, liquidity preference.

preferencial, preferential.

preferente, preferential.

preferido, preferred.

premio, bonus, premium, prize.

— **de cobranza,** collection fee.

— **de seguro,** insurance premium.

prenda, security, collateral.

prescribir, to prescribe.

prescripción, prescription.

presentar al pago, to present for payment.

presidir la asamblea, to preside over the meeting.

prestaciones, benefits.

— **adicionales al sueldo,** fringe benefits.

— **por vejez,** old-age benefits.

prestamista, moneylender.

préstamo, loan.

— **a corto plazo,** short-term loan.

— **bancario,** bank loan.

— **con garantía,** loan against collateral.

— **de consumo,** loan for consumption.

— **de uso,** loan for use.

— **en obligaciones,** loan on debentures.

— **hipotecario,** mortgage loan.

— **personal,** personal loan.

— **reembolsado,** refunded loan.

préstamos a bajo interés, low-interest loans.

prestar, to lend.

— **con respaldo colateral,** to lend on collateral.

— **garantía,** to act as security.

— **sobre hipoteca,** to lend on mortgage.

presupuestar, to estimate.

presupuesto, budget, estimate.

— **aproximado,** rough estimate.

previa deducción de gastos, expenses deducted.

previsión, expectation, foresight.

— **matemática de ganancias,** mathematical expectation of gain.

— **social,** social security, welfare.

previsiones, expectation(s).

previsto, foreseen.

prima, premium.

— **de riesgo,** risk premium.

— **de seguro,** insurance premium.

— **graduada,** sliding-scale premium.

— **matemática,** net premium.

— **única,** single premium.

primer gravamen, first lien.

primera de cambio, first of exchange.

principal, principal, capital.

principio, principle.

privilegio, privilege.

probabilidad, probability.

— **completa de vida,** complete expectation of life.

— **de sobrevivencia,** probability of surviving.

— **de vida,** life expectancy.

—, **superficie de la,** probability surface.

—, **tasa de,** probability rate.

probable, prospective.

procesar, to process, to manufacture, to prosecute.

proceso, process, processing.

— **contencioso,** lawsuit.

— **de datos,** data processing.

— **indirecto,** roundabout process.

producción, production, output.

— **de utilidad máxima,** best-profit outfit.

— **en masa,** mass production.

— **en proceso,** work in process.

— **marginal,** marginal production.

— **nacional,** national product.

producir, to produce, to yield.

— **intereses,** to bear interest.

productividad, productivity.

— **decreciente,** diminishing productiveness.

productivo, productive, profitable.

producto, product, production.

— **bruto,** gross proceeds.

— **bruto nacional,** gross national product.

— **decreciente,** diminishing return.

— **final,** end product.

— **nacional,** national product.

— **primario,** primary commodity, commodity product.

— **social,** social product.

productor, producer.

productos, goods, products.

— **alimenticios,** foodstuffs.

— **básicos,** staple commodities.

— **de consumo,** consumer goods.

— **del país,** domestic goods, national products.

— **domésticos,** home goods.

— **en proceso,** goods in process.

— **semiacabados,** goods partly processed.

— **terminados,** finished products.

proforma, pro forma.

programa, program, schedule.

— **de trabajo** working program.

programación, programming, planning.

— **anticipada,** preprogramming.

— **económica,** economic planning.

programas de conservación, conservation programs.

progresión por categorías, bracket progression.

prohibición de importación, import ban.

promediar, to average.

promedio, average, mean.

— **anual,** annual average.

— **aritmético,** arithmetical mean.

— **de vida futura,** average life expectancy.

— **variable,** moving average.

promesa de crédito, credit commitment.

promesas, commitments.

promisorio, promissory.

promoción, promotion.

— **de ventas,** sales promotion.

promover, to promote.

pronóstico, forecast.

— **a intervalos variables,** varying-interval prediction.

— **de los productores,** producer's forecast.

— **del mercado,** business forecast.

pronósticos de los productos, producer's forecasts.

pronto pago, prompt payment.

propaganda, advertising, publicity.

propensión, propensity.

— **a ahorrar,** propensity to save.

— **a atesorar,** propensity to hoard.

— **a consumir,** propensity to consume.

— **a invertir,** propensity to invest.

— **marginal a consumir,** marginal propensity to consume.

propiedad, ownership.

— **inmueble,** real estate.

— **literaria,** copyright.

propietario, proprietor.

propuesta, bid.

propuestas selladas, sealed bids.

prorrata, pro rata.

prorratear, to prorate.

prórroga, postponement, respite.

prorrogar el vencimiento, to extend the time.

prospecto, prospectus.

prosperidad, prosperity.

próspero, prosperous, successful.

protección arancelaria, tariff protection.

proteccionista, protectionist.

proteger, to protect.

protesta, protest.

protestar un giro, to protest a draft.

protesto, protest.

provechoso, useful, profitable.

proveedor, supplier.

provisional, provisional, temporary.

provisiones, supplies.

proyectar, to plan, to lay out.

proyecto, project, plan.

— **de contrato,** draft of contract.

— **de publicidad,** advertising program.

— **piloto,** pilot project.
prueba, test, proof.
— **de cotejo,** call-back proof.
— **de significación,** significance test.
— **del producto,** product testing.
— **más poderosa,** most-powerful test.
— **simétrica,** symmetrical test.
— **unilateral,** one-sided test.
pruebas no paramétricas, nonparametric tests.
publicación comercial, business publication.
publicidad, publicity, advertising.
puerto, port, harbor.
— **de destino,** port of destination.
— **de embarque,** port of origin, of shipment.
— **de emergencia,** port of distress.
— **de escala,** port of call.
— **de matrícula,** port of registry.

— **interior,** inner harbor.
— **libre,** free port.
— **terminal,** port of delivery.
puesto, job, employment.
— **a bordo,** free on board (F.O.B.).
— **al costado,** free alongside (F.A.S.).
— **clave,** key position.
pujar, to outbid.
pulgada (pulg.), inch.
punto, point.
— **de arranque,** starting point.
— **de desvanecimiento,** vanishing point.
— **de equilibrio,** break even point.
— **de referencia,** bench mark.
— **de reposo,** resting point.
— **de utilidad máxima,** best profit point.
— **de vista,** standpoint.
— **máximo,** peak.
— **oro,** gold point.
— **parámetro,** parameter point.

Q

quebrar, to fail, to become bankrupt.
queja, complaint.
querella, dispute, complaint.

quiebra, bankruptcy, failure.
— **fraudulenta,** fraudulent bankruptcy.

quincena, half month, fortnight.

quincenal, biweekly, fortnightly.

quinquenio, five-year period.

R

racionamiento, rationing.
racionar, to ratio.
radicar una causa, to bring a suit.
radiodifusión, broadcasting.
radiodifusora, broadcasting station.
raíz cuadrada, square root.
rama, en, raw, crude.
ramo, line of business.
rapidez, speed.
raspadura, erasure.
ratificar, to approve.
ratio, ratio.
razón, ratio.
— de depreciación, depreciation rate.
— de operación, operating ratio.
— de paridad de ingresos, parity income ratio.
— social, firm name, trade name.
reacción, reaction.
— automantenida, self-sustaining reaction.
— en cadena, chain reaction.
reaccionar entre sí, to interact.
reaceptación, reacceptance.

reajuste, readjustment.
— gradual, rolling readjustment.
real, real.
realización por inventario, preinventory sale.
rearrendar, to re-lease.
reasegurador, reinsurer.
reaseguro, reinsurance.
reavalúo, reappraisal, reassessment.
rebaja, rebate, reduction, discount.
— de venta, sale discount.
— por cantidad, quantity discount.
— por pronto pago, cash discount.
rebajar sueldo, to cut a salary.
recargar, to overcharge.
recargo, surcharge, surtax.
— impositivo, surtax.
recaudación, collection.
recaudador de impuestos, collector of taxes.
recepcionista, receptionist.
receso económico, business depression.
rechazar, to reject.

recibir, to receive, to accept.
recibo, receipt.
—, al, on receipt.
reciprocidad comercial, reciprocal trade.
recíproco, reciprocal.
reclamación, claim.
reclamar por daños, to claim damages.
reclutar, to recruit.
recobrar, to recover.
recomendar, to recommend.
recompensar, to remunerate.
reconocer, to acknowledge, to recognize, to honor.
rectificar, to correct, to rectify.
recuento, recount.
— físico, physical inventory.
recuperación de los precios, rally in prices.
recuperación económica, business recovery.
recurrente, recurring.
recursos, resources.
— económicos, financial resources.
— líquidos, liquid resources.
— naturales, natural resources.
redactor, editor.
redescuento, rediscount.
redimible, redeemable.
redimir, to redeem.
rédito, return, interest.
redituar, to produce, to yield.

— interés, to bear interest.
reducción, reduction, cutback.
— básica, basic abatement.
— equilibrada, balanced reduction.
reducciones en el presupuesto, cuts in the budget.
reducir, to reduce.
redundancia, redundancy.
reembolsar, to refund, to repay.
reembolso, refund.
reemplazo, replacement.
refaccionar, to finance.
referencia, reference.
— bancaria, bank reference.
— comercial, trade reference.
reforma, reform.
— arancelaria, tariff reform.
— (de una ley), amendment.
— monetaria, currency reform.
regalía, bonus, royalty.
regalo, present, gift.
regatear, to bargain.
regional, regional, local.
monopolio, regional cartel.
registrado, registered.
registradora, (cash) register.
registrar, to register.
registro, record, file, register.
— de inscripción, inscription register.
— de la propiedad, real-estate record office.

— **demográfico,** registry of vital statistics.

—**, derechos de,** registration fees.

regla, rule.

— **de cálculo,** slide rule.

—**, en,** in order.

reglamentación, regulation.

— **de precios,** price fixing.

— **del trabajo,** labor regulations.

reglamento, rules, regulations.

— **interno,** bylaws.

regulación, regulation.

rehacer, to remake.

reinvertir, to reinvest.

relación, report, list, statement.

relaciones, relations.

— **comerciales,** business connections.

rematador, auctioneer.

remate, auction.

remesa, shipment, remittance.

remisión, remittance.

remitente, shipper, sender.

rémora, drag, hindrance.

remuneración equitativa, adequate compensation.

remunerar, to remunerate, to compensate.

rendimiento, output, yield, return.

— **creciente,** increasing returns.

— **de capital,** return on capital.

— **de obligaciones,** bond yield.

— **decreciente,** diminishing returns.

— **fijo,** fixed income.

rendir interés, to bear interest.

renglón, item, line of business.

renovable, renewable, replaceable.

renovación del capital, capital turnover.

renovar, to renew, to replace.

renta, income, rent, annuity.

— **acumulada,** accrued income.

— **del capital,** interest, return on capital.

— **vitalicia,** life annuity.

rentar, to rent.

renuncia, resignation.

renunciar, to resign.

reordenar, to reorder.

reorganizar, to reorganize.

repagar, to repay.

reparar, to repair.

repartición de costos, cost distribution.

repartir, to distribute.

reparto de utilidades, profit sharing.

repasar, to review.

reponer, to replace, to restore.

reportar, to obtain, to report.

— **una ganancia,** to yield a profit.

— **una pérdida,** to show a loss.

reporte, report.

— **anual,** annual report.

— **de auditoría,** auditor's report.

reposición, replacement.

representación, representation.

representante, representative agent.

representar, to represent.

reproducir, to reproduce.

reprogramar, to reprogram.

repudiar, to repudiate.

repuestos, spares, spare parts.

reputación comercial, commercial standing.

requisitos, requirements, requisites, qualifications.

resarcir, to indemnify.

rescate, redemption.

rescindir, to rescind.

reserva, reserve.

— **de contingencia,** contingent reserve.

— **monetaria,** currency reserve.

— **para accidentes industriales,** industrial-accident-fund reserve.

— **para agotamiento,** reserve for depletion.

— **para amortización,** sinking-fund reserve.

— **para auxilio a empleados,** benefit-fund reserve, relief-fund reserve.

— **para bonificaciones,** allowances reserve.

— **para cuentas incobrables,** reserve for bad debts.

— **para depreciación,** reserve for depreciation.

— **para descuentos,** reserve for discounts.

— **para deudas incobrables,** reserve for bad debts.

— **para fluctuaciones en cambios de moneda,** reserve for exchange fluctuations.

— **para impuestos,** reserve for taxes.

— **para participación de utilidades,** profit-sharing reserve.

— **para pensiones,** pension-fund reserve.

— **para renovación y reposición,** reserve for renewals and replacements.

— **secreta,** secret reserve.

— **superior a lo normal,** reserve above normal.

reservas, reserves.

— **de oro,** gold reserve.

residencia, domicile.

residente, resident.

resistencia, resistance.

— **a comprar,** sales resistance.

— **contra los altos precios,** price resistance.
resolver, to resolve.
responder, to answer, to reply.
— **por,** to vouch for.
responsabilidad, responsibility.
— **directa,** primary liability.
— **económica,** financial liability.
— **ilimitada,** unlimited liability.
— **limitada,** limited liability.
responsable, responsible.
respuesta, answer, reply.
resta, subtraction.
restar, to subtract, to deduct.
restituir, to pay back, to refund.
restricción, restriction, curtailment.
— **del comercio,** restraint of trade.
— **del crédito,** credit restriction.
restriccionista, restrictionist.
—, **muestreo,** restricted sampling.
restringir, to restrain.
resultado, result.
resultar, to result.
resumen, summary, abstract.
resumir, to summarize, to sum up.
retardo, delay.

retasar, to reappraise.
retenido, withheld.
retirar, to withdraw.
— **de la circulación,** to withdraw from circulation.
— **efectivo,** to draw cash.
— **el crédito,** to cancel credit.
retirarse, to withdraw, to retire.
retiro, withdrawal, retirement.
— **en efectivo,** cash withdrawal.
retrasar, to delay.
retrasos, arrears.
retribución, fee, compensation, wages.
retribuir, to pay, to remunerate.
retroactivo, retroactive.
reunión, meeting.
revalidar, to revalidate.
revaluación, revaluation.
revaluar, to reappraise, to revalue.
reventa, resale.
revisar, to inspect, to audit, to check.
revisión, inspection, review.
revocable, revocable.
revocar, to revoke, to repeal, to abrogate.
riesgo, risk, hazard.
— **del comprador,** buyer's risk.
— **del transportador,** carrier's risk.

— **del vendedor,** seller's risk.

— **profesional,** occupational hazard.

riesgos asegurables, insurable risks.

riqueza, wealth, worth.

rompehuelga, strikebreaker.

rotación, rotation.

— **de cultivos,** crop rotation.

— **de mercancía,** merchandise turnover.

rotular, to label, to address.

rúbrica, flourish after signature, title.

ruta, route, routing.

rutina, routine.

S

salario, wages, salary.

— **a destajo,** taskwork wages.

— **básico,** basic wage.

— **de hambre,** starvation wages.

— **diario,** daily wage.

— **igual por trabajo igual,** equal pay for equal work.

— **mínimo,** minimum wage.

— **monetario,** money wage.

— **nominal,** nominal wage.

— **real,** real wages.

salarios por hora, hourly wages.

saldar, to settle, to balance.

— **los libros,** to balance the books.

— **una deuda,** to discharge a debt.

saldo, balance.

— **de apertura,** opening balance.

— **de mercancías,** job lot.

— **migratorio,** balance of migration.

— **residual,** residual balance.

salidas, expenditures.

— **de caja,** cash disbursements.

saliente, outgoing.

salvo error u omisión, errors and omissions excepted.

satisfacer la demanda, to meet the demand.

se renta, for rent.

se vende, for sale.

sección, section, division.

— **comercial,** business district.

secretaria, secretary.

— **particular,** private secretary.

secretaría de estado, ministry.

secretariado, secretariat.

secretario, secretary.

— **adjunto,** assistant secretary.

71

— **de actas,** recording secretary.

— **de correspondencia,** corresponding secretary.

— **de finanzas,** secretary of the treasury.

— **ejecutivo,** executive secretary.

— **general,** secretary-general.

— **interino,** acting secretary.

— **privado,** private secretary.

sede, headquarters.

segunda de cambio, second of exchange.

seguridad, safety, guaranty.

seguro, insurance, safe.

— **a término,** term insurance.

— **aéreo,** airplane insurance.

— **colectivo,** group insurance.

— **contra accidentes,** casualty insurance.

— **contra daño por choque,** collision insurance.

— **contra desfalco,** embezzlement insurance.

— **contra incapacidad,** disability insurance.

— **contra incendio,** fire insurance.

— **contra robo,** burglary insurance.

— **contra todo riesgo,** all-risk insurance.

— **cumulativo,** accumulation insurance.

— **de contingencia,** casualty insurance.

— **de cumplimiento,** performance bond.

— **de fidelidad,** fidelity insurance.

— **de guerra,** war-risk insurance.

— **de salud,** health insurance.

— **de transporte,** transportation insurance.

— **de vejez,** old-age insurance.

— **de viajero,** traveler's insurance.

— **de vida ordinario,** ordinary life insurance.

— **dotal,** endowment insurance.

— **familiar,** family insurance.

— **industrial,** industrial insurance.

— **social,** social insurance, social security.

— **y fianza,** insurance and bond.

selección, selection.

— **al azar,** random selection.

— **con igual probabilidad,** selection with equal probability.

— **con probabilidad arbitraria,** selection with arbitrary probability.

— **con probabilidad proporcional al tamaño,** selection with probability proportional to size.

seleccionar, to pick out, to select.

selectivo, selective.

sello, seal, stamp.

semana, week.

— **comercial,** business week.

— **de nómina,** payroll week.

— **inglesa,** (Monday morning to Saturday noon.)

— **laborable,** work week.

semanal, weekly.

semestral, semiannual.

semiacabado, semifinished.

semimayoreo, jobbing.

semimayorista, jobber.

sentencia judicial, legal decision, court judgment.

separación de empleo, dismissal.

seriado, serial.

serie, en, assembly-line, mass production.

servicio, service.

servicios públicos, public-service utilities.

servidumbre predial, predial servitude.

sesión, session, meeting.

— **de clausura,** closing session.

— **de inauguración,** opening session.

— **extraordinaria,** special meeting.

— **ordinaria,** regular meeting.

— **plenaria,** joint session.

sesionar, to hold a meeting.

siglas, initials.

signatario, signatory.

signo, sign, mark.

— **de división,** division sign ($\div$).

— **de interrogación,** question mark (?).

— **de multiplicación,** multiplication sign ($\times$).

— **de por ciento,** percentage sign ($\%$).

— **igual,** equals sign ($=$).

— **de sumar,** addition sign ($+$).

— **de resta,** subtraction sign ($-$).

sigue carta, letter follows.

sin, without.

— **compromiso,** without obligation.

— **demora,** without delay.

— **fecha,** undated.

— **riesgo,** devoid of risk.

— **reclamar,** unclaimed.

— **valor,** worthless.

sindicato, syndicate, union.

siniestro, accident, disaster, damage.

sistema, system.

— **abierto,** opened system.

— **bancario,** banking system.

— **cerrado,** closed system.

— **de castas,** caste system.

— **de salario incentivo,** incentive wage system.

— **de ventas,** sales policy.

— **impositivo,** system of taxation.

— **métrico,** metric system.

sistemas económicos clásicos, classical economics.

sistematizar, to systematize.

sitio, site.

situación, condition, location.

— **de fondos,** remittance payment.

— **financiera,** financial standing.

sobornar, to bribe.

soborno, graft.

sobrante, surplus.

sobre la par, above par.

sobrecarga, overload.

sobrecosto, additional charge.

sobreflete, freight surcharge.

sobregiro, overdraft.

sobreimpuesto, surtax.

sobreinversión, overinvestment.

sobreprecio, surcharge, excess price.

sobrepujar, to outbid.

sobreseer, to supersede.

sobrestante, foreman.

sobretasa, surtax.

sobretiempo, overtime.

sobreutilidad, excess profits.

socialismo, socialism.

sociedad, society, association.

— **anónima,** corporation.

— **cerrada,** close corporation.

— **civil,** civil partnership.

— **de ahorro y préstamo,** savings and loan association.

— **de crédito,** credit institution.

— **de responsabilidad limitada,** limited-liability company.

— **en comandita por acciones,** joint-stock company.

— **familiar,** family partnership.

— **filial,** subsidiary company.

— **financiera,** finance company.

— **inversionista,** investment trust.

— **matriz,** parent company.

socio, member, partner.

— **activo,** active partner.

— **capitalista,** partner who furnishes capital only.

— **industrial,** partner who furnishes services only.

— **menor,** junior partner.

— **principal,** senior partner.

socios fundadores, founding stockholders.

solicitante, applicant.

— **de préstamo,** loan applicant.

solicitar, to apply for.

— **empleo,** to look for a job.

solicitud, application, petition.

—, a, on request.

— **de cotización,** request for quotation.

— **de empleo,** application for employment.

— **de préstamo,** loan application.

solución, solution, settlement.

solvencia, ability to pay, solvency.

— **económica,** financial responsibility.

solvente, solvent, sound.

someter, to submit.

sorteo, drawing by lot.

sostener el precio, to keep up the price.

sostenimiento, support, maintenance.

subagencia, subagency.

subalterno, subordinate.

subarrendar, to sublet.

subarriendo, sublease.

subasta, auction.

subastar, to auction.

subcomisión, subcommittee.

subdesarrollado, underdeveloped.

subdirector, assistant manager, associate director.

subdividir, to subdivide.

submuestra, subsample.

subnormal, subnormal, substandard.

subproducto, by-product, subproduct, residual product.

subrayar, to underscore.

subsanar, to adjust.

subscribir, to subscribe, to underwrite.

subscriptor, subscriber.

subscrito, signed, subscribed.

subsidiar, to subsidize.

subsidio, subsidy.

— **de precios,** price subsidy.

substituir, to substitute.

substracción, subtraction.

substraer, subtract.

subtotal, subtotal.

subunidad, subunit.

sucesión, succession, estate.

sucesores, successors.

sucursal, branch.

sueldo, salary, wages.

—, a, on a salary.

— **base,** basic wage rate.

sueldos acumulados, accrued salaries.

sufragar los gastos, to meet the costs.

sujetarse a condiciones, to meet conditions.

sujeto, person, subject.

— **a aprobación,** on approval.

— **a impuesto,** taxable.

suma, addition, amount.

— **a la vuelta,** carry-over.

— **total,** grand total.

— **y sigue,** amount carried forward.

sumadora, adding machine.
sumar, to add.
sumario, summary, abstract.
suministrar, to furnish.
suntuario, luxury, sumptuary.
superabundancia, glut.
superar, to surpass, to exceed.
superávit, surplus.
superconsumo, excessive consumption.
superficialmente, perfunctorily.
supermercado, supermarket.
superproducción, overproduction.
supervisar, to supervise.
supervisor, overseer, supervisor.
supervivencia, survival.
suplemento, supplement.
suplente, substitute.

suplir, to supplement, to substitute.
suprimible, abatable.
suprimir, to cancel, to suppress, to abolish.
supuesto, assumption.
surtir un pedido, to fill an order.
suscripción, subscription.
suscriptor, subscriber, signer.
suscrito, undersigned, subscribed.
susodicho, above-mentioned.
suspender, to discontinue, to interrupt.
— pago, to stop payment.
— un pedido, to hold up an order.
sustento, support, maintenance.
sustituto, substitute.

T

tabla, table.
— de la demanda, demand schedule.
— de mortalidad actual, current life table.
tablas, tables.
— de grupos humanos, cohort tables.
— de mortalidad de generaciones, generation life tables.

tabulación de datos, tabulation of data.
tabulador de sueldos, wage scale.
tabular, tabulate.
tachar, to strike out, to delete.
táctica financiera, financial policy.
taller, shop.
talón, stub, coupon.
— oro, gold standard.

— **postal,** postal receipt.

talonario, stub book.

— **de cheques,** checkbook.

tamaño, size.

— **medio de las familias,** mean size of family.

tanteo, approximate estimate.

taquigrafía, shorthand, stenography.

taquígrafo, a, stenographer.

taquimecanógrafo, a, stenographer-typist.

tara, tare.

— **real,** actual tare.

— **según factura,** invoice tare.

— **tasada,** estimated tare.

— **y merma,** tare and tret.

tarar, to weigh before loading, to tare.

tarea, piecework, job.

tarifa, tariff, fare.

— **arancelaria,** schedule of customs duties.

— **base,** base rate.

— **de favor para los miembros del Commonwealth,** imperial preference.

— **del cambio,** rate of exchange.

— **diurna,** date rate.

— **fiscal,** schedule of import duties.

— **postal,** postal rates.

— **preferencial,** preferential tariff.

— **proteccionista,** protective tariff.

— **única,** flat rate.

tarjeta, card.

tasa, rate, tax.

— **básica,** base rate.

— **de crecimiento,** rate of growth.

— **de depreciación,** depreciation rate.

— **de descuento,** discount rate.

— **de interés,** rate of interest.

— **de mortalidad,** death rate.

— **de mortalidad por profesiones,** occupational death rate.

— **de nacimiento,** birth rate.

— **de probabilidad,** probability rate.

— **de rendimiento,** rate of return.

— **impositiva,** tax rate.

— **media,** average rate.

— **real,** effective rate.

— **uniforme,** flat rate.

tasable, ratable.

tasación, appraisal, assessment, rating.

tasar, to appraise, to assess.

tecla, key.

teclado, keyboard.

técnica, technique.

— **comercial,** marketing.

técnico, expert, technician.

tecnológico, technological.

tendencia, trend.

— **alcista,** upward trend.

— **demográfica,** population trend.

tendencias, tendencies, trends.

— **del mercado,** market trends.

— **en conflicto,** conflicting tendencies.

— **inflacionistas,** inflationary trends.

tenedor, holder.

— **de acciones,** stockholder.

— **de libros,** bookkeeper.

— **de póliza,** policyholder.

— **de títulos,** security holder.

teneduría de libros, bookkeeping.

tenencia, holding, possession.

teoría, theory.

— **de costos,** theory of comparative costs.

— **de los valores internacionales,** theory of international values.

tercería, arbitration, intervention.

término, term, deadline.

— **de entrega,** time of delivery.

— **medio,** average.

términos de venta, terms of sale.

terrateniente, landholder, landowner.

terreno, land, ground. lot.

territorio reservado, exclusive territory.

tesorería, treasury.

tesorero, treasurer.

testificar, to witness, to testify.

testigo, witness, specimen, sample.

texto, text.

tiempo, time, term.

— **doble,** double time.

— **extra,** overtime.

— **muerto,** dead time.

— **perdido,** lost time.

— **y medio,** time and a half.

tiendas en cadena, chain stores.

tierra, earth, land.

— **de labor,** cultivated land.

— **de riego,** irrigated farm land.

— **de temporal,** unirrigated farm land.

— **virgen,** virgin soil.

timar, to swindle.

timbre, stamp, seal.

— **fiscal,** revenue stamp.

— **postal,** postage stamp.

tipo, standard, type, kind.

— **bancario,** bank rate.

— **básico,** normal rate.

— **corriente,** current rate.

— **de cambio,** conversion rate.

— **de descuento,** discount rate.

— **de interés,** interest rate.

— **medio de aumento,** average of increase.

tipos cruzados, cross rates.
tiraje, edition, issue.
tiro, edition, circulation.
titulado, certified, licensed.
titular, holder (of a department), official.
título, title, right, article.
— **al portador,** bearer instrument.
— **constitutivo,** charter.
— **de compraventa,** bill of sale.
— **de patente,** letters patent.
— **de propiedad,** title deed.
— **hipotecario,** mortgage bond.
— **minero,** mining claim.
títulos, securities, documents.
— **fiduciarios,** bonds.
todo riesgo, all risks.
tolerancia, tolerance, allowance.
tomador de tiempo, timekeeper.
tomar, to take.
— **a préstamo,** to borrow.
— **dictado,** to take dictation.
— **en arriendo,** to lease, to rent.
— **la palabra,** to take the floor.
— **nota,** to take notice.
— **parte en,** to take part in.
— **un pedido,** to take an order.
tonel, barrel.

tonelada, ton.
— **corta,** short ton.
— **larga,** long ton.
— **métrica,** metric ton.
tonelaje, tonnage.
total de prueba, proof total.
totalidad, full amount.
totalizador, totalizer.
trabajador, laborer, worker.
— **a domicilio,** homeworker.
— **a jornal,** wageworker.
— **a sueldo,** salaried employee.
— **calificado,** skilled workman.
— **de oficina,** office worker, white-collar worker.
— **del campo,** farm hand.
— **eventual,** casual worker.
— **no sindicalizado,** non-union workman.
trabajadores eventuales, casual workers.
trabajo, work, job.
— **a destajo,** piecework, taskwork.
— **de oficina,** clerical work.
— **de urgencia,** rush work.
— **diurno,** daytime work.
— **en proceso,** work in process.
— **en serie,** assembly-line operation.
— **extraordinario,** overtime work.
— **infantil,** child labor.

— **manual,** manual labor.
traducción, translation.
traducir, to translate.
traductor, translator.
tráfico, traffic.
tramitar, to carry out, to negotiate.
trámite, step, procedure.
—, en, pending.
transacción, transaction, settlement.
transar, to settle, to compromise.
transbordar, to transship.
transcribir, to transcribe.
transferencia, transfer.
transferible, transferable.
transigir, to compromise.
tránsito, transit, traffic.
transitorio, temporary.
transmitir, forward.
transportación, transportation.
transportador, carrier.

transportar, to carry.
transporte, transportation.
traspasar, to assign, to transfer.
traspaso, assignment, cession.
— **de título de propiedad,** change of title.
tratado, treaty, agreement.
— **comercial,** trade agreement.
trato, deal, agreement.
tribunal, court.
tributación, taxation.
— **fiscal,** federal tax.
— **graduada,** graduated taxation.
— **por timbre,** stamp tax.
— **por utilidades,** income tax.
— **progresiva,** progressive taxation.
tributo, tax, contribution.
trimestre, quarter.
triplicado, triplicate.
trueque, barter.

U

ubicación, site, location.
ultramar, overseas.
unánime, unanimous.
unidad, unity, unit.
— **de costo,** cost unit.
— **de cuenta,** accounting unit.
— **de trabajo,** labor unit.

— **marginal,** marginal unit.
— **monetaria,** unit of currency, monetary unit.
uniformar, to standardize.
unilateral, unilateral.
unión, union, merger.
unionismo, unionism.
unitario, unitary.

uso, use, custom, practice.
— **final,** end use.
— **y desgaste,** wear and tear.
usuario, user.
usufructo, usufruct.
usurero, usurer.
utilidad, profit, usefulness.
— **accidental,** casual income.
— **bruta,** gross profit.
— **creciente,** increasing returns.
— **de forma,** form utility.
— **de lugar,** place utility.
— **de tiempo,** time utility.
— **decreciente,** diminishing returns.
— **gravable,** taxable profit.
— **líquida,** net profit.
— **marginal,** marginal utility.
— **neta,** net profit.
— **unitaria,** unit profit.
utilidades, earnings, profit.
— **acumuladas,** accumulated profits.
— **antes de los impuestos,** pretax earnings.
— **anticipadas,** anticipated profits.
— **aparentes,** book profits.

— **brutas,** gross profits.
— **contingentes,** contingent profits.
— **de las empresas,** corporate earnings.
— **de operación,** operating profit.
— **devengadas,** accrued income.
— **diferidas,** deferred income, deferred credits.
— **esperadas,** anticipated profits.
— **excedentes,** excess profits.
— **gravables,** taxable profits.
— **netas,** net profits.
— **no realizadas,** paper profits.
— **no repartidas,** undistributed profits.
—, **ocultación de,** concealment of profits.
— **realizadas,** realized profits.
— **reinvertidas,** reinvested profits.
— **repartibles,** distributive profits.
— **según libros,** book profits.
utópico, utopian.

V

vacante, vacancy, vacant.
vale, voucher, promissory note (I.O.U.).

— **de caja chica,** petty-cash voucher.
valer, to cost, to be worth.

valía, worth, value.
validar, to validate.
válido, valid.
valioso, valuable.
valor, value, price.
— **a la par,** par value.
—, **al,** ad valorem.
— **al cobro,** value for collection.
— **al vencimiento,** value at maturity.
— **actual,** present value.
— **agregado,** value added.
— **asignado,** rating.
— **catastral,** assessed valuation.
— **convenido,** agreed value.
— **de costo,** cost value.
— **de emisión,** issue price.
— **de factura,** invoice value.
— **de venta,** selling price.
— **depreciado,** depreciated value.
— **en cambio,** exchange value.
— **en libros,** book value.
— **en plaza,** market value.
— **global,** aggregate value.
— **entendido,** value agreed upon.
— **justo del mercado,** fair market value.
— **líquido,** net value.
— **nominal,** face value, nominal value.
— **ponderado,** weighted value.

— **recibido,** value received.
— **total,** aggregate value.
valores, securities, assets.
— **a recibir,** receivables.
— **al cobro,** receivables.
— **bancarios,** bank paper.
— **bursátiles,** stock-exchange securities, listed securities.
— **de renta fija,** fixed-income securities.
— **de renta variable,** common stocks.
— **del estado,** government bonds.
— **en cobranza,** bills for collection.
— **fiscales,** government bonds.
— **hipotecarios,** mortgage bonds.
— **materiales,** physical assets.
— **valorización,** appraisal, valuation.
valorizar, to appraise, to value.
valuable, ratable, appraisable.
valuación, valuation, appraisal.
valuador, appraiser.
valuar en menos, to undervalue.
variable, variable.
— **aleatoria continua,** continuous random variable.
— **dependiente,** dependent variable.

— **vectorial aleatoria,** vector random variable.

variables independientes, independent variables.

variación, variation, variance.

— **del promedio,** variance from the average.

— **del tipo,** variation from standard.

— **entre grupos,** between groups variance.

variancia interbloque, inter-block variance.

velocidad, speed.

— **de giro,** turnover.

— **del dinero,** velocity of money.

velocidad-ingreso del dinero, income - velocity of money.

vencer, to mature, expire.

vencido, overdue.

vencimiento, maturity, maturity date, expiration.

vendedor, salesman, seller.

— **a domicilio,** canvasser, peddler.

— **mayorista,** wholesaler.

— **viajero,** traveling salesman.

vender, to sell.

— **a comisión,** to sell on commission.

— **al contado,** to sell for cash.

— **al mayoreo,** to sell at wholesale.

— **al menudeo,** to sell at retail.

— **con pérdida,** to sell at a loss.

— **en descubierto,** to sell short.

— **en remate,** to auction.

véndese, for sale.

vendibilidad, salability.

vendible, salable.

venta, sale.

— **a plazos,** installment selling.

— **al contado,** cash sale.

— **al descubierto,** short selling.

— **de balance,** inventory sale.

— **de liquidación,** clearance sale.

— **de oportunidad,** bargain sale.

— **en almoneda,** auction sale.

— **forzosa,** forced sale.

— **incondicional,** absolute sale.

— **judicial,** foreclosure sale.

ventaja, advantage.

ventas

— **a crédito,** charge sales.

— **al detalle,** retail sales.

— **de puerta en puerta,** door-to-door selling.

— **en abonos,** installment sales.

— **netas,** net sales.

verificar, to verify, to check.

— **el protesto,** to protest.
— **un censo,** to take a census.
vetar, to veto.
vía, route, way.
viaje, travel, trip.
— **de negocios,** business trip.
— **redondo,** round trip.
— **sencillo,** one-way trip.
— **sin escala,** nonstop trip.
viajero, passenger, traveler.
— **comerciante,** traveling salesman.
viáticos, traveling expenses.
vicio, defect, flaw.

vigencia, duration.
violación de contrato, breach of contract.
visita, call, visit.
vista de aduana, customs inspector.
vocal, member of a board.
volumen, volume.
votación, voting.
votar, to vote.
veto, vote.
— **de calidad,** deciding vote.
— **de confianza,** vote of confidence.
vuelo, flight.

Y

yarda (yd), yard.

yarda cuadrada, square yard.

Z

zona, zone, district, area.
— **comercial,** business district, shopping center.
— **de influencia,** sphere of interest.
— **de ventas,** sales territory.

— **del dólar,** dollar area.
— **libre,** free zone.
— **postal,** postal zone.
— **residencial,** residential neighborhood.

English–Spanish
Inglés–Español

A

abalienate, to, enajenar, traspasar.

abalienation, enajenación, traspaso.

abandonment, abandono.

abatable, rebajable.

abate, to, rebajar, suprimir, reducir-se.

abatement, supresión, rebaja, reducción.

abeyance, suspensión, expectativa.

—, in, en suspenso, pendiente.

ability to pay, solvencia.

abolish, to, suprimir, anular, derogar.

above par, sobre la par.

abridge, to, abreviar, resumir.

abrogate, to, revocar, anular.

absenteeism, absentismo, ausentismo.

absolute, absoluto.

— endorsement, endoso absoluto.

— interest, interés establecido.

— sale, venta incondicional.

— total loss, pérdida total.

absorb the loss, to, asumir la pérdida.

abstract, resumen, sumario.

accelerated depreciation, depreciación acelerada.

acceleration, aceleración

— clause, cláusula para el vencimiento anticipado de una deuda.

— note, pagaré con opción de pago adelantado.

— principle, principio de aceleración.

accept, to, aceptar, reconocer, comprometerse a pagar un documento.

— subject to, aceptar a reserva de.

acceptance, aceptación.

— agreement, contrato de aceptación.

— bill, letra aceptada.

— credit, crédito de aceptación.

—, trade, aceptación comercial.

acceptor, aceptante, aceptador.

accidental damage, daño, deterioro accidental.

accommodation, favor, ajuste, arreglo.

— **credit,** crédito en descubierto, de favor.

— **endorsement,** endoso por aval.

accommodations, facilidades.

accord (*n*.) acuerdo, convenio; (*v*.) conceder.

account, cuenta.

—, **balance,** cuenta de balance.

—, **current,** cuenta corriente.

—, **drawing,** cuenta corriente.

— **for, to,** dar razón de.

—, **on,** a cuenta.

— **stated,** cuenta conforme, convenida.

accountable, responsable, contable.

accountant, contador, contable.

accounting, contabilidad, contaduría, rendición o preparación de cuentas.

— **standards,** normas contables, normas de contabilidad.

accounts, cuentas.

—, **nominal,** cuentas impersonales.

—, **payable,** cuentas por pagar.

— **receivable,** cuentas por cobrar.

—, **secured,** cuentas garantizadas.

accretion, acrecentamiento, acumulación.

accrual, acumulación.

— **basis,** base acumulativa, contabilidad por acumulación.

accrue, to, acumular, resultar.

accrued, acumulado.

— **charges,** cargos acumulados.

— **interest,** interés acumulado.

— **taxes,** impuestos causados, vencidos, por pagar.

accumulated random series, serie aleatoria acumulada.

accumulative error, error cumulativo.

accuracy, precisión.

acid-test ratio, proporción entre el activo y pasivo circulante.

acknowledge, to, admitir, reconocer.

— **receipt,** acusar recibo.

acquire, to, adquirir.

acquired rights, derechos adquiridos.

acre, acre (0.405 hectárea).

act, (*n*.) acto, hecho, derecho; (*v*.) actuar.

— **of incorporation,** escritura constitutiva.

acting, interino, suplente.

— **manager,** gerente interino, suplente.

active, activo.

— **account,** cuenta activa, en actividad corriente.

— **assets,** activo productivo.

— **debt,** deuda que produce interés.

— **partner,** socio activo.

— **trust,** fideicomiso activo.

activity analysis, programación lineal.

actual, efectivo, real, verdadero.

— **basis,** gastos reales.

— **behavior,** conducta real.

— **cash value,** valor real en el mercado, costo de reposición.

— **cost,** costo efectivo.

— **employment,** ocupación real.

— **income,** ingreso efectivo.

— **loss,** pérdida efectiva.

— **market value,** valor real en el mercado, en plaza.

— **price,** precio verdadero, real.

— **relationship,** relación verdadera.

— **wage,** salario efectivo.

— **yield,** rendimiento real.

actuarial

— **estimate,** estimación actuarial.

— **profit,** ganancia contable.

actuary, actuario.

ad valorem, ad valorem, según valor.

addressee, destinatario.

adequate compensation, compensación, remuneración equitativa.

adjust, to, regularizar, tasar, ajustar.

adjusted rate, tasa ajustada.

adjustment, arreglo, ajuste, tasación.

— **of a claim,** pago de una reclamación.

administered prices, precios controlados (por el gobierno) o fijados por un monopolio.

administration expenses, gastos de administración.

administrative agency, oficina administrativa (del gobierno).

administrator, administrador, dirigente.

admitted assets, activo computable, admitido.

advance, anticipo, adelanto.

— **bill,** letra, factura, giro, enviados antes del embarque.

— **deposit,** depósito anticipado.

—, **in,** por adelantado.

— **notice,** aviso anticipado.

— **payment,** pago adelantado.

advances, anticipos, adelantos, préstamos.

adventure, empresa, especulación, riesgo.

—, joint, especulación en participación.

adverse change, cambio desfavorable.

advertisement, anuncio.

advertising, propaganda, publicidad.

— agency, agencia de publicidad.

— budget, presupuesto para publicidad.

— expenses, gastos de publicidad.

— value, valor publicitario.

advice, aviso, notificación.

advisable, aconsejable, conveniente, recomendable.

advise, to, avisar, notificar.

advisory, consultivo.

— committee, comité consultivo.

— council, consejo consultivo, consejo de asesoramiento.

affairs, statement of, estado estimado de liquidación.

affect, to, afectar, hipotecar.

affected, afectado.

affidavit, declaración, testimonio ante notario público, acta notarial.

affiliated company, compañía, empresa asociada, filial.

age, edad.

— at entry, edad de ingreso.

— at withdrawal, edad de retiro.

— composition of population, composición de la población por edad.

— group, grupo de edad.

— mean, edad media, promedio de edad.

—, of, mayor de edad.

—, under, menor de edad.

age-adjusted, ajustado según edad.

agency, agencia, órgano.

agenda, orden del día.

agent, agente, representante.

aggregate, global, total, agregado.

— demand function, función de la demanda global.

— demand price, precio de la demanda global.

— employment, ocupación global.

— gross liabilities, pasivo bruto global.

— imports, total de importaciones, importaciones globales.

— investment, inversión total.

— product, producto global.

— real wage, monto total de salarios reales.

— supply function, función total de la oferta.

— **supply of labor,** oferta total de mano de obra.

— **supply price,** precio de la oferta global.

— **volume,** volumen total.

aggregates, cantidades globales.

aggresive, dinámico.

aging of accounts, análisis de la antigüedad de las cuentas.

agio, agio.

agreement, contrato, arreglo.

aid, ayuda.

aimed-at precision, precisión propuesta.

aimed-at sampling error, error de muestreo propuesto.

air, aire.

— **express,** expreso aéreo.

— **freight,** carga aérea.

aleatory, aleatorio.

alien, extranjero.

— **corporation,** compañía, sociedad anónima de otra nación.

alienable, enajenable.

alienate, to, enajenar, transferir.

allocation, asignación, cuota, distribución, aplicación.

allot, to, repartir, distribuir.

allotment, asignación, cuota.

allowance, bonificación, descuento, rebaja, tolerancia.

amalgamation, amalgama, fusión.

amend, to, enmendar, reformar, corregir.

amendment, reforma (de una ley).

American Federation of Labor (A.F. of L.) Federación Americana del Trabajo.

amortization, amortización.

— **factor,** coeficiente de amortización.

— **schedule,** programa, cuadro de amortización.

amount, monto, importe, suma.

— **due,** suma debida.

ancillary letter of credit, carta de crédito auxiliar.

annual, anual.

— **report,** informe anual.

— **statement,** estado anual.

— **value,** rendimiento, valor anual (de terrenos agrícolas).

annuity, anualidad, pensión o renta anual.

— **benefits,** beneficios de pensión.

— **bond,** bono sin vencimiento.

— **contract,** contrato de pensión, de anualidad.

—**, deferred,** anualidad diferida.

—**, life,** anualidad vitalicia.

— **payable,** anualidad pasiva.

annul, to, anular, cancelar.

anomalous endorsement, endoso irregular.

antagonistic cooperation, cooperación por necesidad, no de buen grado.

anticipated profits, utilidades previstas anticipadas.

antidumping duty, impuesto para evitar el "dumping".

antimonopoly, antimonopolista.

antitrust laws, leyes antimonopolistas, opuestas a los carteles.

appeal, to, apelar.

applicant, solicitante.

application, solicitud.

applied demography, demografía aplicada.

apply, to, aplicar, solicitar gestionar.

appoint, to, nombrar.

apportion, to, prorratear, repartir.

apportionment, prorrateo, distribución, derrama.

appraisal, valuación, tasación.

— of precision, valuación de la precisión.

appraise, to, apreciar, tasar, valuar.

appraisement, valuación, tasación.

appreciation, alza, apreciación.

appropriation, asignación, aplicación, suma presupuestada.

arbitration, arbitraje.

area, área, zona.

— comparability factor, factor de comparabilidad de áreas.

—, depressed, zona de crisis económica.

— sampling, muestreo de zona, basándose en subdivisiones de la misma.

areas, major producing, principales zonas productoras.

arrears, atrasos, retrasos.

— of interest, intereses atrasados.

articles of partnership, contrato de asociación.

assay, ensayo (de minerales).

assembly-line technic, sistema de producción en serie.

assenting securities, valores de tenedores consencientes.

assess, to, tasar, valuar.

assessed valuation, avalúo catastral.

assessment, tasación, avalúo, gravamen.

assets, activo, bienes.

—, accrued, activo acumulado.

—, admissible, activo computable.

92

— **and liabilities,** activo y pasivo.

—, **available,** activo realizable.

—, **capital,** activo fijo.

—, **cash,** activo disponible.

—, **circulating,** activo circulante.

—, **contingent,** activo contingente.

—, **current,** activo circulante.

—, **deferred,** activo diferido.

—, **doubtful,** activo dudoso.

—, **fixed,** activo fijo.

—, **foreign,** activo en el extranjero.

— **in hand,** bienes disponibles.

—, **interest yielding,** bienes, activo con rendimiento de interés.

—, **liquid,** activo de fácil realización.

—, **nonproductive,** activo improductivo.

—, **physical,** activo tangible.

—, **working,** activo circulante.

assign, to, asignar, aplicar.

assignee, cesionario.

assimilation, asimilación (de valores bursátiles por parte del público).

assistance payment, pago de ayuda o asistencia.

associate, socio, asociado.

associated company, compañía, empresa afiliada.

association, sociedad, compañía, asociación.

assumption, supuesto.

asymtotical, asintótico.

atomistic society, sociedad de economía en la que predominan las unidades productoras pequeñas.

attorney, abogado, procurador.

— **general,** procurador general, ministro fiscal general.

auction, subasta, remate, subastar.

— **sale,** subasta, venta en almoneda.

audit, (*n.*) auditoría; (*v.*) auditorear.

—, **balance sheet,** auditoría de balance.

—, **cash,** auditoría de caja.

— **procedure,** procedimiento de auditoría.

—, **public,** auditoría pública.

— **report,** informe de auditoría.

auditing standards, normas de auditoría.

auditor, auditor, interventor.

austerity program, política (nacional) de austeridad, de economía.

authenticate, to, autenticar, refrendar, legalizar.

authorized, autorizado.
— **capital,** capital autorizado.
— **signature,** firma autorizada.
automatic wage adjustment, ajuste automático de sueldos.
automation, automatismo, automatización, cambio técnico al sistema automático.
available, disponible.
— **labor,** mano de obra disponible.

— **resources,** recursos disponibles.
average, promedio, término medio, promediar.
— **adjuster,** arreglador, tasador, ajustador.
— **balance,** saldo medio.
— **price,** precio medio.
— **sample number,** número muestral promedio.
— **unit cost,** cost unitario promedio.
— **variable cost,** costo variable promedio.

B

back taxes, impuestos atrasados.
backlog, acumulación, reserva.
bad debts, cuentas incobrables.
bail, fianza.
bailee, depositario.
balance, (*n.*) saldo, balance, diferencia; (*v.*) balancear, igualar.
— **of international payments,** balanza de pagos.
— **of migration,** saldo migratorio.
— **of trade,** balanza comercial.
— **sheet,** balance general.
balanced reduction, reducción equilibrada.

balanced sample, muestra contrabalanceada.
balancing factor, factor de compensación.
bank, banco.
— **acceptance,** aceptación bancaria.
— **account,** cuenta bancaria.
— **branch,** sucursal de banco.
— **clearings,** compensaciones bancarias.
— **draft,** letra, giro bancario.
— **examiners,** auditores, inspectores bancarios.
— **money order,** giro bancario.
— **note,** billete de banco.

— **of issue,** banco que emite billetes de banco.

— **overdraft,** sobregiro real.

— **papers,** valores bancarios.

— **rate,** tasa bancaria.

— **reconciliation,** conciliación bancaria.

— **reserves,** reservas bancarias.

— **return,** estado bancario.

—, **savings,** caja de ahorros.

—, **statement,** estado bancario, extracto de cuenta.

— **syndicate,** consorcio bancario.

bankable, descontable.

banker's acceptance, aceptación bancaria.

banking, banca, bancario.

—, **company,** sociedad bancaria.

— **department,** departamento bancario.

— **house,** institución bancaria.

— **system,** sistema bancario.

bankrupt, to go, quebrar, hacer quiebra.

bankruptcy, quiebra, bancarrota.

bargain, (n.) ganga, barata; pacto, convenio; (v.) negociar.

bargaining, trato, convenio, regateo.

— **power,** poder para negociar.

barren money, dinero que no produce interés.

barrier, barrera.

barter, (n.) trueque, intercambio de mercancías; (v.) trocar.

— **agreements,** convenios de trueque.

— **trade,** comercio de trueque, de operaciones compensadas.

basic, básico.

— **abatement,** reducción básica.

— **crops,** cultivos básicos.

— **investment,** inversión básica.

— **patent,** patente primitiva, original.

— **rebate,** descuento básico.

— **stock,** existencia mínima.

— **supplementary cost,** costo suplementario básico.

basis, base.

— **for depreciation,** base de depreciación.

— **of assessment,** base de avalúo.

— **of taxation,** base del impuesto.

basket bidding, licitación sobre varios valores a la vez.

bear sale, venta especulativa a la baja.

bear speculator, especulador a la baja.

bearer, portador, tenedor.

— **bond,** bono o título al portador.

— **debenture,** obligación al portador.

— **paper,** documento al portador.

— **securities,** títulos al portador.

— **share,** acción al portador.

bears, bajistas.

beginning inventory, existencia inicial.

behavior, comportamiento.

—, **actual,** conducta actual.

—, **price,** comportamiento de los precios.

beneficiary, beneficiario, tenedor, portador.

benefit, provecho, beneficio.

— **society,** sociedad de beneficencia.

berthage, amarraje, derechos de atraque.

best, mejor.

— **bid,** la mejor oferta.

— **profit output,** producción de utilidad máxima.

— **profit point,** punto de utilidad máxima.

between groups variance, variación entre grupos.

between-jobs, entre empleos sucesivos.

bias, bias, parcialidad, predisposición, prejuicio.

bid, oferta, postura, ofrecer, pujar, licitar.

— **and offer,** demanda y oferta.

— **in, to,** sobrepujar para beneficiar al vendedor.

— **up, to,** aumentar la oferta.

bidder, highest, mejor postor.

bilateral agreement, acuerdo bilateral.

bill, (*n.*) factura, cuenta, letra, giro, billete; (*v.*) facturar.

— **of entry,** declaración aduanal.

— **of exchange, inland,** letra de cambio interna.

— **of lading (B/L),** conocimiento de embarque.

— **of sale,** escritura de venta, factura.

bills, facturas, documentos.

— **due,** documentos vencidos, por pagar.

— **payable,** documentos por pagar.

— **receivable,** documentos por cobrar.

bimetallism, sistema monetario bimetálico, bimetalismo (llamado también **"double standard"**).

binding agreement, acuerdo obligatorio.

birth, nacimiento.

— **control,** control de natalidad.

— **rate,** natalidad, tasa de natalidad.

black Friday, cualquiera de los viernes históricos en que ocurrieron desastres financieros.

black market, mercado negro.

blank, en blanco.

— **acceptance,** aceptación en blanco.

blanket bond, fianza general, colectiva.

— **policy,** póliza abierta.

block of stocks, lote de acciones.

blocked, bloqueado, controlado, congelado.

— **account,** cuenta bloqueada, controlada, congelada.

— **currency,** moneda controlada, con limitaciones en el mercado internacional.

— **funds,** fondos congelados.

blue chips, valores, acciones de primera.

board, junta directiva.

— **meeting,** sesión de los directivos.

— **of audit,** junta de auditoría, de revisión.

— **of customs,** administración de aduanas.

— **of directors,** junta directiva, dirección.

— **of equalization,** junta de revisión de avalúos.

Board of Trade (G.B.), Ministerio de Comercio.

bond, (*n.*) bono, título; (*v.*) dar fianza.

— **and mortgage,** escritura de préstamo e hipoteca.

— **company,** compañía de fianzas.

—, **debenture,** bono sin garantía hipotecaria.

—, **in,** afianzado, en admisión temporal, en aduana.

—, **interest,** bono para pagar intereses de otros bonos.

— **issue,** emisión de bonos.

—, **mortgage,** bono con garantía hipotecaria.

— **of indemnity,** fianza de indemnización.

—, **registered,** bono nominativo, bono registrado (a nombre del dueño).

—, **registered coupon,** bono registrado a nombre del dueño con cupones al portador.

—, **revenue,** bono respaldado con ingresos públicos especiales.

—, **saving,** bono de ahorro, título de ahorro.

bonded, afianzado.

— **carrier,** empresa transportadora afianzada.

— **goods,** mercancías admitidas bajo fianza.

— **warehouse,** depósito aduanal, bodega fiscal.

bondholder, tenedor de bonos.

bondholdings, bonos en cartera.

bonding company, compañía de fianzas.

bondsman, fiador, afianzador.

bonus, premio, bonificación, prima.

— **share,** acción gratuita, beneficiaria.

book, libro.

— **entry,** asiento (contable), partida.

— **of original entry,** libro de primera entrada, libro diario.

— **value,** valor según libros.

bookkeeping, teneduría de libros.

boom, período de auge, bonanza.

bootleg, ilícito, ilegal.

borrow, to, tomar en préstamo, pedir prestado.

bottleneck, embotellamiento, estrangulamiento.

bounty, bonificación, prima.

boycott, (*n.*) boicot; (*v.*) boicotear.

bracket progression, progresión por categorías.

branch, sucursal.

brand, marca de fábrica.

branded goods, artículos de marca.

breadwinner, asalariado, sostén de la familia.

break, to, quebrar, arruinarse.

break even point, punto o momento sin utilidad ni pérdida, punto de equilibrio.

break even, to, cubrir los gastos, lograr un equilibrio entre pérdidas y ganancias.

breakdown, análisis, descomposición.

bribe, (*n.*) soborno; (*v.*) sobornar.

bring into conformity, to, hacer coincidir.

broad market, período de movimiento (compra-venta) de gran variedad de acciones.

broker, corredor, agente.

brokerage, corretaje.

budget, (*n.*) presupuesto; (*v.*) presupuestar.

— **accounts,** cuentas de presupuesto.

— **administration,** administración del presupuesto.

— **allocation,** asignación del presupuesto.

— **allotment,** distribución del presupuesto.

— **appropriation,** asignación del presupuesto.

—**authorization,** autorización del presupuesto.

— **balance,** equilibrio del presupuesto.

—**deficit,** déficit presupuestal.

— **estimates,** cálculo, proyecto del presupuesto.

— **price,** precio módico.

budgetary cuts, reducciones del presupuesto.

budgetting, preparación del presupuesto.

buffer pool, reserva, fondo estabilizador, amortiguador.

buffer stock, reserva, fondo, almacenamiento estabilizador.

— **plan,** política de existencias estabilizadoras.

build up capital, to, crear capital.

built-in, integrante.

bulk, grueso, bulto, volumen.

— **cargo,** mercancías transportadas en granel.

—**, in,** a granel, sin envase, suelto, en bruto.

bull speculator, especulador al alza.

bullion reserve, reserva metálica, (oro y plata).

bulls, alcistas.

buoyant prices, precios con tendencia al alza.

burden, gravamen, gravar, imponer cargas excesivas.

bureau, oficina, agencia, dirección.

bushel (bu.), fanega (E.U.: 35.238 l.).

business, negocios, comercio, transacciones comerciales.

— **contraction,** contracción del mercado.

— **cycle,** ciclo económico.

— **deal,** transacción comercial, negocio.

— **deposits,** depósitos para gastos de consumo.

— **district,** zona comercial.

— **earnings,** utilidades de la empresa.

— **expansion,** expansión del mercado.

—**forecast,** pronóstico del mercado.

— **house,** establecimiento comercial.

— **income,** ingresos comerciales o industriales.

— **investment,** inversión comercial.

— **motive,** motivo negocios.

— **profits,** utilidades comerciales.

— **recession,** depresión económica.

— **recovery,** recuperación económica.

— **statistics,** estadísticas comerciales.

— **trend,** tendencia del mercado.

buy, to, comprar.

— **at wholesale,** comprar al por mayor.
— **on installments,** comprar en abonos, a plazos.
— **up,** acaparar.
buyer, comprador, agente de compras.

buyers' market, mercado del consumidor, favorable al consumidor.
buying up, acaparamiento.
by-product, derivado, subproducto.
bylaws, estatutos secundarios.

C

cadastre, catastro.
calendar year, año civil.
calibrating factor, factor para rectificar.
call, (*n.*) visita, comunicación, retiro; (*v.*) llamar, retirar.
— **date,** fecha de reembolso.
— **loan,** préstamo reembolsable a la vista.
— **money,** dinero prestado exigible a la vista.
— **off, to,** dar por terminado.
callable bond, bono reembolsable con anticipación.
calling in of currency, retiro de moneda.
canons of taxation, estipulaciones en política impositiva.
capacity (of a plant or equipment) capacidad de producción.
capital, capital.
— **account,** cuenta de capital.
— **assets,** activo fijo, bienes de capital.

—, **authorized,** capital autorizado.
— **budget,** presupuesto de gastos de capital.
—, **circulating,** activo circulante.
—, **consumption,** capital de consumo.
— **deficiencies,** penuria, deficiencia de capital, insuficiencia de equipo.
— **development fund,** fondos para equipo de producción.
— **dividend,** dividendo de capital.
— **equipment,** bienes de equipo productor.
— **expenditures,** gastos de capital.
—, **fixed,** activo fijo.
—, **floating,** capital circulante o flotante.
— **flow,** movimiento de capital.
— **formation,** formación de capital.

100

— **gains,** utilidades de capital, ganancias por enajenación de bienes.

— **gains tax,** impuestos sobre las ganancias de capital.

— **goods,** bienes de capital, de equipo, de producción.

— **inflow,** afluencia de capital.

—, **instrumental,** capital instrumental.

—, **invested,** capital invertido.

— **investment,** inversión de capital.

—, **issued,** capital emitido.

— **levy,** impuesto sobre capital.

— **liabilities,** pasivo fijo, obligaciones de capital.

— **loss,** pérdida de capital.

— **market,** mercado de capitales, mercado financiero.

—, **nominal,** capital social.

—, **original,** capital original.

— **outflow,** salida de capitales al exterior.

—, **paid-in,** capital exhibido.

— **payment,** pago de cuenta de capital.

—, **registered,** capital autorizado.

— **resources,** bienes de equipo, infraestructura.

— **share,** acción de capital.

— **stock,** capital social (de sociedad por acciones), acciones de capital.

— **stock tax,** impuesto sobre capital en acciones.

—, **subscribed,** capital suscrito.

— **surplus,** excedente de capital.

— **transactions,** transacciones de capital.

— **transfer,** transferencia de capital.

— **turnover,** movimiento, rotabilidad de fondos.

—, **uncalled,** capital suscrito, pero no exhibido.

—, **unproductive,** capital improductivo.

—, **watered,** capital inflado.

—, **working,** capital en giro, activo circulante, capital de trabajo.

capital-goods industries, industrias de artículos (bienes) de capital.

capitation tax, impuesto por persona, capitación.

cargo insurance, seguro de mercancía.

cargo liner, barco de carga.

carrier, empresa transportadora.

carrier's risk, riesgo del transportador.

carry-back, pérdida traspasada al año anterior.

carry-over, pérdida traspasada al año siguiente, saldo anterior.

cartage, acarreo.

cartel, cartel, monopolio.

cartelized commodity, producto cartelizado, controlado por cartel.

cash, (*n.*) efectivo; (*v.*) hacer efectivo.

— **and carry,** pago al contado con transporte a cargo del comprador.

— **at (in) (with) bank,** efectivo en el banco.

— **balance,** saldo de caja.

— **basis,** al contado.

— **book,** libro de caja.

— **control record,** libro de caja.

— **count,** arqueo de caja.

— **deal,** operación al contado.

— **deficit,** déficit de caja.

— **discount,** descuento por pronto pago.

— **economy,** economía monetaria.

— **funds,** fondos en efectivo.

— **holdings,** disponibilidades en efectivo.

— **imprest,** fondo fijo de caja.

— **in hand,** efectivo disponible, existencia en caja.

— **journal,** libro, diario de caja.

— **leakage,** merma en efectivo.

— **on delivery (C.O.D.),** por cobrar, contra reembolso. (También **collect on delivery.**)

— **outgo and income,** entradas y salidas de caja.

— **payment,** pago al contado.

—, **petty,** caja chica, de menores.

— **position,** situación líquida.

— **price,** precio al contado.

—, **ready,** disponibilidades de caja.

— **reserves,** reservas líquidas en efectivo.

— **sale,** venta al contado.

— **shorts and overs,** déficits y excedentes de caja.

— **value,** valor efectivo.

— **voucher,** comprobante de caja.

cashier, cajero.

cashier's check, cheque de caja, de ventanilla.

caste system, sistema de castas.

casual income, utilidad accidental.

casual workers, trabajadores eventuales.

ceiling price, precio tope.

center of location, centro de ubicación.

centigram (cg), centigramo.

centiliter (cl), centilitro.

centimeter (cm), centímetro.

centrally planned economy, economía dirigida.

certificate, certificado, dictamen, reporte, acta, certificar.

— inventory, confirmación de inventario.

— of conformity, certificado de conformidad.

— of deposit, certificado de depósito.

— of indebtness, certificado de adeudo.

— of origin, certificado de origen.

—, qualified, certificado con salvedades.

—, unqualified, certificado sin salvedades.

certified, certificado.

— bill of lading, conocimiento de embarque con certificación consular.

— check, cheque certificado.

— public accountant, contador público titulado.

certify, to, certificar, dar fe.

chair, presidente, ponente.

chairman of the board, presidente del consejo.

chamber of commerce, cámara de comercio.

change, (n.) cambio; (v.) cambiar.

— in costs, cambio en los costos.

— in expectation, cambio en las previsiones.

character loan, préstamos sin garantía colateral.

charge, (n.) cargo; (v.) cargar, cobrar.

— account, cuenta corriente, abierta.

chargeable, cargable, adeudable.

charges, cargos, débitos, gastos.

— collect, gastos por cobrar.

—, deferred, cargos diferidos.

—, overhead, sobrecarga, gastos indirectos.

charitable trust, fideicomiso caritativo.

charter, (n.) escritura de constitución de una corporación, contrato de fletamiento de un barco; (v.) fletar, constituir.

chartered, autorizado, contratado.

cheat, to, engañar, estafar.

check, (n.) cheque, comprobación; (v.) comprobar, revisar.

—, cash, cheque de caja.

— clearings, compensaciones de cheques, compensaciones bancarias.

— data, datos comprobatorios.

— list, lista de verificación, de comprobación.

— **stub,** talón de cheque.

— **to bearer,** cheque al portador.

—, **traveler's,** cheque de viajero.

— **up, to,** cotejar, confrontar, verificar.

checking account, cuenta de cheques, de depósito.

checks, cheques.

— **for collection,** cheques al cobro.

—, **outstanding,** cheques pendientes.

—, **returned,** cheques, devueltos.

cheque (Brit.), cheque (*véase* check).

child labor, trabajo de menores.

C.I.F. (cost, insurance and freight), costo, seguro y flete.

circulating, circulante.

— **assets,** activo circulante, en rotación.

— **capital,** capital circulante, en explotación.

claim, (*n.*) reclamación, demanda; (*v.*) reclamar, demandar.

— **adjuster,** ajustador de reclamaciones.

— **damage, to,** reclamar por daño.

— **established,** reclamación reconocida.

— **for short delivery,** reclamación por envío incompleto.

class struggle, lucha de clases.

classical economics, sistemas económicos clásicos.

clause, cláusula, disposición.

clean, limpio, sin reservas, simple.

— **acceptance,** aceptación general.

— **bill of exchange,** letra limpia, sin reservas.

— **bill of lading,** conocimiento de embarque sin observaciones.

— **credit,** crédito simple.

— **draft,** letra o giro simple, sin colaterales.

— **profit,** beneficio líquido.

— **value,** valor líquido.

clearance, despacho aduanal, compensación (bancaria).

— **inwards,** declaración de entrada (en aduana).

— **outwards,** declaración de salida (de aduana).

— **sale,** venta de liquidación.

clearing, compensación.

— **agreement,** convenio de compensaciones.

— **association,** asociación de compensación.

— **balance,** saldo no compensado.

— **house,** cámara de compensación.

clearings, compensaciones bancarias.

close corporation, sociedad anónima controlada por pocos.

closed, cerrado.

— **account,** cuenta saldada.

— **bids,** propuestas selladas.

— **market,** mercado reservado, exclusivo.

— **union,** gremio obrero que hace muy difícil la entrada a nuevos miembros.

closing of accounts, cierre de cuentas (al final del ejercicio).

closing price, precio de cierre.

coasting trade, cabotaje, comercio costero.

code, (*n.*) código; (*v.*) codificar.

codrawer, cogirador.

coefficient, coeficiente.

— **of apportionment,** coeficiente de repartición.

— **of elasticity,** coeficiente de elasticidad.

— **of variation,** coeficiente de variación.

cohort, grupo humano.

— **analysis,** análisis de grupos humanos.

— **tables,** tablas de grupos humanos.

coin money, (*n.*) moneda fraccionaria; (*v.*) acuñar moneda.

collapse of prices, caída, desplome de precios.

collapse, to, derrumbarse.

collateral, colateral, garantía, resguardo.

— **acceptance,** aceptación de garantía.

— **contract,** contrato de prenda.

— **loan,** préstamo con garantía.

— **note,** pagaré prendario, colateral.

— **security,** garantía prendaria, colateral.

collect, to, cobrar, recaudar.

collected, cobrado, colectado.

collection, cobro, recaudación.

— **agency,** compañía, agencia de cobranzas.

— **expenses,** gastos de cobranza.

— **items,** efectos por cobrar.

collective bargaining, contratación colectiva, convenio colectivo.

collector of customs, administrador de aduana.

collector of internal revenue, recaudador de rentas.

collisions, tropiezos.

combination in restraint of trade, acuerdo para restringir la competencia.

combine, cartel, unión de organizaciones o empresas, consorcio.

commerce, comercio.

commercial, comercial, mercantil.

— **code,** código comercial, derecho mercantil.

— **grades,** calidades comerciales.

— **invoice,** factura comercial.

— **law,** derecho mercantil.

— **papers,** documentos negociables, usualmente a corto plazo.

— **usage,** costumbres comerciales, usos comerciales.

— **value,** valor en plaza, de mercado.

commission, comisión.

— **agent,** agente a comisión, comisionista.

— **basis,** a comisión.

— **merchant,** comisionista.

—, **on,** a comisión.

—, **selling,** comisión de ventas.

commitment, compromiso.

committee, comité, junta.

commodity, artículo, mercancía, producto.

— **agreement,** acuerdo sobre mercancías.

— **arbitrage scheme,** plan de arbitraje sobre mercancías.

— **arrangements,** acuerdos sobre mercancías.

— **exchange,** bolsa de productos.

— **flow,** corriente de mercancías.

— **hoarding,** acaparamiento de mercancías.

— **index number,** número índice de (cada) mercancía.

—, **luxury,** artículo de lujo, producto suntuario.

— **management,** reglamentación en materia de productos.

— **paper,** efectos respaldados por productos.

—, **primary,** artículo básico.

— **rates,** tarifas para mercancías.

— **standard,** mercancía patrón.

Common European Market, Mercado Común Europeo.

common, común.

— **ownership,** condominio, propiedad en común.

— **share,** acción común, ordinaria.

— **stock,** acciones comunes, ordinarias.

Commonwealth, British, Comunidad Británica de Naciones.

company, compañía, socie-
dad, corporación, empresa.
—, affiliated, compañía filial.
—, allied, compañía asociada.
—, controlled, compañía filial.
— deeds, actas de la sociedad.
—, holding, compañía matriz,
principal, propietaria de las
acciones.
—, merged, compañía fusionada.
—, parent, compañía matriz,
principal o propietaria.
—, stock, compañía por acciones.
— union, sindicato formado
por empleados de una sola
compañía.
compensating error, error
de compensación.
compensation, compensa-
ción, remuneración, indemnización.
compensatory duty, impuesto compensatorio (como de-
fensa de la industria nacional).
compensatory financing, financiamiento compensato-
rio, financiación compensa-
toria.
competitive price, precio de
competencia.
completed products, pro-
ductos terminados.

completion, terminación, término.
comply with allotments, to,
quedar dentro de los límites
de asignaciones fijadas.
component method, método
de los componentes.
component of standard of
living, elemento del nivel
de vida.
composite commodity, mer-
cancía compuesta.
composite hypothesis, hi-
pótesis compuesta.
composition in bankruptcy,
acuerdo, arreglo entre falli-
do y acreedores.
compound interest, interés
compuesto.
comprehensive economic
control, control económico
comprensivo.
compression of demand,
compresión de la demanda.
comptroller, contralor.
compulsory, obligatorio.
— arbitration, arbitraje obligatorio.
— purchase, compra obli-
gatoria, expropiación.
— reserves of banks, reservas bancarias obligatorias.
— return, declaración obligatoria.
— sale, venta obligatoria, expropiación.

computation, cálculo, estimación, avalúo, evaluación.

computer, computador.

concealment of profits, ocultación de utilidades.

concern, empresa, casa comercial.

concession, concesión, privilegio.

— in price, precio especial, rebajado.

concessionaire, concesionario.

conciliation board, junta de conciliación.

condemnation, expropiación. enajenación obligatoria.

conditional endorsement, endoso condicional.

conference, conferencia, sindicato, consorcio.

confiscatory taxation, tributación confiscatoria.

conflict, conflicto, oposición,

conflicting tendencies, tendencias en conflicto.

Congress of Industrial Organizations (C.I.O.), Congreso de Organizaciones Industriales. (Actualmente unida a la **American Federation of Labor (A.F. of L.).**

consequential damages, daños emergentes.

conservation programs, programas de conservación.

consideration, precio, prestación.

consignee, destinatario, consignatario.

consignment, consignación.

consignor, remitente.

consolidate, to, consolidar, unir, combinar.

consolidated, consolidado.

— amount, monto global.

— balance sheet, estado de contabilidad consolidado.

— budget, presupuesto global.

— business income, cuenta consolidada de ingreso.

— cash position, situación de caja global.

— debt, deuda consolidada.

consolidating of a tariff, consolidación de una tarifa.

consolidating statement, estado de consolidación.

consolidation, consolidación, concentración.

conspicuous consumption, consumo debido a lo visible del precio y llamativo del producto.

constant currency, moneda de valor constante.

constant percentage depreciation method, método de amortización de porcentaje constante.

consular, consular.

— fees, derechos consulares.

— **invoice,** factura consular.

consumables, bienes consumibles.

consumer credit, crédito del consumidor.

consumer-purchaser, consumidor-comprador.

consumers' goods, bienes de consumo.

consumer's price index, índice de precios de mercancías de consumo.

consumption, consumo.

— **duties,** derechos de consumo.

— **function,** función consumo.

consumption-goods industries, industrias de artículos de consumo.

contingency, eventualidad.

— **fund,** fondo para imprevistos.

contingent, eventual, contingente.

continuing guaranty, garantía continua.

continuous, continuo.

— **population register,** registro continuo de la población.

— **random variable,** variable aleatoria continua.

contract, (*n.*) contrato, convenio, escritura; (*v.*) contratar.

— **bond,** fianza de contratista.

— **carrier,** empresa transportadora por contrato.

— **labor,** trabajadores, braceros contratados (de otro país).

— **of affreightment,** póliza de fletamiento.

— **of hire,** contrato de trabajo, de empleo.

— **of sale,** contrato de compraventa.

— **price,** precio acordado según contrato.

— **time,** lapso de terminación.

—, **under,** bajo contrato.

contracting parties, partes contratantes.

contracyclical policy, política anticíclica.

control board, junta de control.

controlled, controlado, dirigido.

— **company,** compañía filial.

— **economy,** economía dirigida.

— **exchange,** cambio controlado; ver **"exchange control".**

— **prices,** precios controlados, regulados.

— **sample,** muestra controlada.

controller, controlador, contralor.

controlling interest, participación de control, inversión dominante.

conversion, conversión, canje.

convertible, convertible.

— **assets,** activo convertible.

conveyance, título de traspaso, de traslación de dominio.

co-owner, copropietario.

copyright, derechos de reproducción, derechos de autor.

corporate, incorporado, social.

— **body,** sociedad anónima.

— **bond,** bono, obligación de una sociedad.

— **business,** empresa constituida en sociedad.

— **capital,** capital social.

— **name,** razón social.

— **profits,** utilidades de sociedad anónima.

— **saving,** ahorro social.

— **taxes,** impuestos de sociedad anónima.

— **trust,** fideicomiso de sociedad anónima.

corporation, sociedad anónima por acciones.

cost, costo.

— **accounting,** contabilidad de costos.

— **analysis,** análisis de costos.

—, **carrying,** costo de almacenamiento.

—, **competitive,** precio de competencia.

— **control,** control de costos.

— **curves,** curvas de costo.

—, **direct,** costos directos.

— **distribution,** repartición de costos.

—, **factor,** costo de factores.

—, **fixed,** costo fijo.

— **function,** función del costo.

—, **historical,** costo inicial.

—, **increased,** aumento del costo.

—, **indirect,** costos indirectos, sobrecarga, gastos indirectos.

— **insurance and freight (C. I.F.),** costo, seguro y flete.

— **insurance, freight and exchange (C.I.F. and E.),** costo, seguro, flete y cambio.

— **of living,** cost de la vida.

— **of living differential,** tasa diferencial del costo de la vida.

—, **operating,** costo de producción.

— **or market, whichever is lower,** el menor precio, ya sea de costo o de mercado.

—, **standard,** costo tipo.

—, **user,** costo de uso.

cost-plus contract, costo más honorarios.

counteract, to, contrarrestar.

counterclaim, contrademanda.

counterfeit, falsificación.

— **money,** dinero falso.

counterfoil, talón.

countervailing, compensatorio.

country bank, banco rural.

coupon bonds, bonos al portador.

court, tribunal, juzgado.

credit, (*n.*) crédito; (*v.*) acreditar.

— **against taxes,** deducción por impuestos pagados.

— **balance,** saldo acreedor.

— **bank,** banco de crédito.

— **buying,** compras a crédito.

— **control,** control de créditos.

—, **deferred,** crédito diferido.

— **instrument,** documento o instrumento de crédito.

—, **letter of,** carta de crédito.

— **note,** nota de crédito.

—, **on,** a crédito.

—, **open,** crédito abierto.

— **policy,** política de crédito.

— **rating,** grado o límite de crédito (de una negociación).

— **references,** referencias de crédito.

— **report,** informe de crédito.

— **statement,** estado financiero (en relación con los créditos).

— **underwriters,** aseguradores de crédito.

creditor, acreedor.

creditors, sundry, acreedores diversos.

credits, frozen, créditos congelados.

critical materials, materiales estratégicos.

crop, cosecha, producción agrícola.

— **correspondents,** corresponsales agrícolas.

— **index,** índice, coeficiente de producción agrícola.

— **insurance,** seguro contra la pérdida de las cosechas.

cross licensing, concesión recíproca de licencias, de derechos de patente.

cross section, corte representativo.

cubic foot (ft³), pie cúbico (28.317 dm³).

cubic meter (m³), metro cúbico.

cum rights, acciones con derecho a la compra de otras de nueva emisión.

cumulative, acumulativo, acumulable.

— **dividend,** dividendo acumulable.

— **preferred stock,** acciones privilegiadas de dividendo acumulable.

curb exchange, bolsa de valores (desde 1953 tomó el nombre de **American Stock Exchange**).

currency, moneda de un país.

— **area,** zona monetaria.

— **devaluation,** devaluación de la moneda.

—, **foreign,** divisas, moneda extranjera.

—, **hard,** divisas convertibles, estables.

current, corriente.

— **account,** cuenta corriente.

— **assets,** activo corriente, en rotación.

— **expectations,** previsiones actuales.

— **expenditures,** gastos corrientes.

— **input,** insumo corriente.

— **liabilities,** pasivo, circulante, exigible.

— **life table,** tabla de mortalidad actual.

— **physical output,** producción física corriente.

— **price,** precio corriente del mercado.

— **revenue,** ingreso ordinario.

— **services,** servicios habituales.

— **supplementary cost,** costo suplementario actual.

— **surplus,** excedente, superávit de operación.

— **value,** valor actual, precio corriente.

— **yield,** rendimiento corriente.

curtailment, restricción.

custom of trade, usanza, costumbre de plaza.

customer, cliente.

customhouse, aduana.

customs

— **appraiser,** vista aduanal.

— **bond,** fianza de aduana.

— **bonded,** bajo control aduanal.

— **broker,** agente aduanal.

— **clearance,** despacho aduanal.

— **declaration,** declaración aduanal.

— **duty,** derechos de aduana.

— **manifest,** manifiesto de aduana.

— **rebate,** rebaja en los derechos de aduana.

— **receipts,** ingresos de aduana.

— **regulations,** reglamento de aduana.

— **tariffs,** aranceles aduanales.

— **union,** unión, asociación de aduanas.

— **value,** valor en aduana.

customs-exempt, exento de derechos aduanales.

cut, (*n.*) rebaja; (*v.*) cortar, reducir.

cybernetics, cibernética.

cycle, ciclo.

cyclical fluctuations, fluctuaciones cíclicas.

D

daily, diario, cotidiano.

damage, daño, deterioro, avería.

— survey, inspección de avería.

data, datos.

date of delivery, fecha de entrega.

date, out of, caducado.

dated bond, bono a plazo fijo.

day laborer,(Brit.),labourer, jornalero, peón, bracero.

days of grace, días de gracia (para pagar una deuda).

dead freight, falso flete.

dead weight capacity, tonelaje.

deadline, término, límite del plazo fijado.

deadlock, estancamiento.

deal, (n.) negociación, operación, transacción; (v.) negociar

dealer, distribuidor, negociante.

death duties, impuestos de sucesión.

death rate, mortalidad, tasa de mortalidad.

death tax, impuestos de sucesión.

debasement, depreciación de la moneda por rebaja en el contenido metálico.

debenture, obligación, título de crédito, orden de pago.

—, floating, obligaciones flotantes.

— issue, emisión de obligaciones.

—, mortgage, obligaciones de hipoteca.

—, simple, obligaciones simples, sin garantía específica.

debit, cargo, débito, adeudar, cargar.

— balance, saldo deudor.

— deferred, cargo diferido.

debt, deuda, adeudo, obligación.

— at sight, deuda a la vista.

—, floating, deuda flotante.

—, funded, deuda consolidada.

debtor, deudor.

debts, bad, cuentas malas, deudores morosos.

decagram (dag), decagramo.

decaliter (dal), decalitro.

decameter (dam), decámetro.

decigram (dg), decigramo.

deciliter (dl), decilitro.

decimeter (dm), decímetro.

declaration of trust, declaración de fideicomiso.

declared capital, capital declarado, escriturado.

declining balance method, método de amortización decreciente.

decline (*n.*) baja; (*v.*) bajar.

decreasing employment, baja de la ocupación.

deductible, deducible.

deduction, deducción, descuento.

deed, escritura, contrato.

— of gift, escritura de donación.

— of sale, contrato de compraventa.

— of transfer, escritura de traspaso.

— of trust, escritura de fideicomiso.

defalcation, desfalco.

defective goods (merchandise), mercancías defectuosas.

deferred, diferido.

— annuities, anualidades, rentas diferidas o aplazadas.

— assets, activo diferido.

— bond, bono de interés diferido.

— charges, cargos diferidos.

— liabilities, pasivo diferido.

— payment, pago aplazado.

deficiency payment, pago para cubrir un déficit.

deficit

— economy, economía deficitaria.

— financing, financiamiento deficitario.

— spending, gastos deficitarios.

deflate, to, desinflar.

deflated, deflacionado, reducido.

deflation, deflación.

degree, grado.

degressive taxation, imposición degresiva.

delinquent return, declaración tardía.

delinquent tax, impuesto no pagado a tiempo.

delivery, entrega, despacho.

— bond, fianza para devolver bienes embargados.

—, future, entrega futura.

delivery, date of, fecha de entrega.

demand (*n.*) demanda; (*v.*) mandar, cobrar.

— bill, letra, giro a la vista.

— curve, curva de la demanda.

— deposits, depósitos a la vista.

— draft, letra, giro a la vista.

— for labor, demanda de trabajadores, de mano de obra.

— note, pagaré a la vista.

—, on, a la presentación, a la vista.

— schedule, tabla, curva de la demanda.

114

demarcation dispute, conflicto intergremial sobre responsabilidades.

demurrage, demora.

denounce, to, denunciar, dar por terminado.

density, densidad.

— function, función de densidad.

dependent, dependiente.

— contract, contrato condicional.

— variable, variable dependiente.

deplete, to, agotar.

depletion, agotamiento.

deposit, (*n.*) depósito; (*v.*) depositar.

— account, cuenta de depósito, cuenta corriente.

—, derivative, depósito derivado.

—, on, en depósito, en el banco.

deposits, business, depósitos para gastos de negocio.

deposits, savings, depósitos de ahorro.

depreciation, depreciación.

—, accrued, depreciación acumulada.

— allowance, reserva de depreciación, amortización permitida.

—, composite, depreciación combinada.

— cost, costo de depreciación.

— of currency, depreciación de la moneda.

—, straight line, depreciación en línea recta.

depressed prices, precios rebajados.

depressing influence, influencia depresiva.

deration, to, suspender el racionamiento.

deterioration, deterioro, evolución desfavorable.

devaluation, devaluación.

development fund, fondo de expansión.

devise, to, idear.

digital computer, computador electrónico (digital).

diminishing, decreciente.

— balance, amortización decreciente.

— productiveness, productividad decreciente.

— returns, rendimiento decreciente.

direct, directo.

— collection, cobro directo.

— investment, inversión directa.

— sale, venta directa.

— tax, impuesto directo.

disability income, ingreso, renta por incapacidad.

disburse, to, desembolsar.

discontinue, to, descontinuar, suspender.

discount, (*n.*) descuento, bonificación; (*v.*) descontar.

— bank, banco de descuento.

—, cash, descuento por pronto pago.

— factor, factor de descuento.

— house, institución de descuento.

— policy, sistema de descuento.

— price, precio de descuento, precio rebajado.

— rate, tasa, tipo de descuento.

discrepancy, discrepancia, diferencia.

discrimination, discriminación.

discriminatory assistance, ayuda preferente.

dishonor, to, no aceptar, no pagar.

dishonored bill, letra rechazada.

disinvest, to, disminuir la inversión.

dismissal wage, indemnización por despido.

dispatch, expedición, envío.

dispense with, to, renunciar a.

disposable income, ingreso disponible, neto.

disposal, disposición, cesión.

dispose of, deshacerse de una cosa.

disposition, aplicación, arreglo disposición.

dispute, conflicto.

—, labor, conflicto de trabajo.

disqualified, incapacitado, incompetente.

dissaving, ahorro negativo, (gastos mayores que los ingresos).

dissenting stockholders, accionistas disidentes.

distort, to, distorcionar, tergiversar, falsear.

distress, remate, urgencia.

— budget, presupuesto reducido, limitado.

— prices, precios de remate.

— selling, ventas de urgencia.

distribution census, censo de distribución.

distributive tax, impuesto de repartición.

disutility, desutilidad (cuando la utilidad de un artículo se convierte en negativa).

diversion of profits, desviación ilícita de utilidades.

divest, to, despojar.

dividend, dividendo.

— arrears, atrasos de dividendo.

—, cash, dividendos en efectivo.

—, declared, dividendo decretado.

—, deferred, dividendo diferido.

— in kind, dividendo en especie.

—, **interim,** dividendo parcial.

—, **liquidating,** dividendo de liquidación.

—, **passed,** dividendo omitido.

—, **preferred,** dividendo preferente.

—, **stock,** dividendos en acciones.

—, **unclaimed,** dividendo no reclamado.

— **warrant,** cédula de dividendo.

dock, muelle.

— **charges,** derechos de atraque, de muelle.

— **receipt,** guía, recibo de muelle.

— **warehouse,** almacén de aduana.

— **warrant,** conocimiento de almacén de aduana.

document, (*n.*) documento, acta; (*v.*) documentar.

documents, documentos.

—, **against,** contra documentos.

— **against payment,** documentos contra pago.

— **for collection,** documentos por cobrar.

dole, socorro pecuniario o en especie dado por el gobierno a cesantes.

dollar, dólar.

— **area,** zona del dólar.

— **gap,** déficit de dólares.

— **shortage,** escasez de dólares.

domestic, nacional, del país.

— **bill,** letra sobre el interior.

— **commerce,** comercio nacional, interior.

— **commodities,** productos nacionales.

— **concerns,** empresas nacionales.

— **currency,** moneda del país.

— **debt,** deuda interior.

— **investment,** inversión interior.

— **market,** mercado nacional.

— **product,** producto nacional.

domicile, domicilio, residencia.

donate, to, donar, contribuir.

donation, donación.

donor, donador.

double, doble.

— **damages,** indemnización doble.

— **entry,** partida doble.

— **indemnity,** doble indemnización.

— **liability,** doble responsabilidad.

— **standard,** talón, patrón doble.

— **taxation,** doble tributación.

double-dealing, falsedad, engaño.

down period, período de cierre (de una fábrica) por reparaciones.

down-swing, fase descendente.

down-turn, receso económico, fase de depresión.

draft, (n.) giro, letra de cambio; (v.) redactar.

—, bank, giro bancario.

—, sight, giro a la vista.

—, time, giro a plazo.

drag, (n.) rémora; (v.) avanzar lentamente.

draw, to, girar.

— a bill, girar una letra.

— a check, extender un cheque.

— interest, producir intereses.

drawback, devolución.

drawee, girado, librado.

drawer, girador.

drive, campaña publicitaria.

drop of prices, caída de precios, baja del mercado.

dry cargo vessel, barco de carga seca.

dry trust, fideicomiso pasivo.

due, vencido, pagadero.

— date, fecha de vencimiento.

— on demand, pagadero a la vista.

dues, cuotas, derechos.

dull market, mercado flojo, inactivo.

dummy directors, directores provisionales.

dumping, "dumping" (inundación del mercado con mercancía de bajo precio).

—, hidden, dumping encubierto.

duopoly, duopolio.

durable goods, bienes duraderos.

durable manufacture, manufactura de bienes duraderos.

dutiable, gravable.

duty, impuesto derechos.

duty-free, exento de impuestos.

dwindle, to, disminuir.

E

earmarked, reservado.

— gold, oro en consignación, en custodia.

— sale, venta reservada.

— for, destinado a.

earned, ganado, devengado.

— income, ingreso devengado.

— interest, interés devengado, acumulado.

— **surplus,** beneficios acumulados.

earnings, ingresos, utilidades, ganancias.

—, **gross,** ganancias brutas.

—, **net,** utilidades netas.

— **statement,** estado de ganancias (y pérdidas).

easement, servidumbre.

easy, fácil.

— **market,** mercado en calma.

— **money,** mercado fácil de dinero, crédito fácil.

— **payments,** facilidades de pago.

— **terms,** facilidades de pago.

economic, económico, de economía.

— **cycle,** ciclo económico.

— **determinism,** determinismo económico (la evolución social como resultado de las fuerzas económicas).

— **development,** desarrollo económico.

— **flow,** corriente económica.

— **growth,** crecimiento económico.

— **pattern,** estructura económica.

— **planning,** planeación, programación económica.

— **policy,** política económica, sistema económico.

— **warfare,** guerra económica.

economics, economía.

—, **classical,** economía clásica.

—, **consumer,** aspectos económicos del consumo.

—, **welfare,** economía para el bienestar social.

economy of abundance, economía de abundancia.

economy of scarcity, economía de escasez.

economy, one crop, economía de monocultivo.

effect payment, to, efectuar el pago.

effective, efectivo.

— **demand,** demanda efectiva.

— **depreciation factor,** factor real de la demanda.

— **rate,** tasa real.

effects, bienes, efectos.

elastic demand, demanda elástica.

elasticity of supply, elasticidad de la oferta.

embargo, (*n.*) embargo, prohibición; (*v.*) embargar.

embezzle, to, desfalcar.

embezzlement, desfalco.

emergency fund, fondo, reserva para casos imprevistos.

eminent domain, dominio, derecho eminente (del gobierno).

employ, (*n.*) empleo; (*v.*) emplear.

employable population, población susceptible de tomar empleo.

employee, empleado.

employer, patrón, empresario.

employment, empleo, contrato de trabajo.

—, actual, ocupación real.

— agency, agencia de colocaciones.

—, full, empleo total.

—, full-time, empleo, jornada de horario completo.

— function, función de empleo.

— index number, índice de ocupación.

— multiplier, multiplicador de ocupación.

—, part-time, empleo, jornada reducida.

enclosure, anexo.

encumbrance, gravamen, carga.

end of period, fin del ejercicio.

end product, producto final.

endeavor, esfuerzo, esforzarse.

endogenous change, alteración en la vida económica debido a factores económicos.

endorsable, endosable.

endorse, to, endosar.

endorsement, endoso.

endow, to, dotar.

endowment, dote, fundación.

— policy, póliza dotal.

enforcement, ejecución de una ley.

enlarge, to, aumentar.

enroll, to, inscribir, inscribirse.

entente, convenio, pacto.

enterprise, empresa.

entrepreneur, empresario.

entry, entrada, asiento, anotación.

—, blind, asiento confuso.

—, books of original, libros de primera entrada.

—, cash, asiento de caja.

—, credit, asiento de abono.

—, cross, asiento cruzado.

—, debit, asiento de cargo.

—, ledger, asiento de mayor.

— permit, permiso de entrada, de declaración aduanal.

equal pay for equal work, igual remuneración por igual trabajo.

equalization fund, fondo de estabilización, caja de compensación.

equate, to, igualar.

equated date, fecha media de vencimiento.

equilibrium, equilibrio.

— in competition, equilibrio en la competencia.

— level of employment, nivel de equilibrio de la ocupación.

— **profit,** ganancia normal, de equilibrio.

— **value,** valor de equilibrio.

equipment, equipo.

— **bond,** bono sobre equipo.

— **trust,** escritura fiduciaria sobre equipo.

equitable, equitativo.

equities, acciones (ordinarias).

error, error.

— **band,** zona de error.

— **in surveys,** error en encuestas.

— **of first kind,** error de primera especie.

— **reducing power,** potencia de reducción del error.

— **weight function,** función de ponderación del error.

escalator clause, cláusula sobre el tipo graduable de salario, de alquiler, etc.

escape clause, cláusula de escape.

estate, propiedad, cuerpo de la herencia.

— **agent,** corredor de bienes raices.

— **in common,** propiedad mancomunada.

— **tax,** impuesto sobre sucesiones.

estimate, (*n.*) estimación, presupuesto; (*v.*) presupuestar.

estimated ratio, razón estimativa.

estimates, cálculos, estimaciones.

evade, to, evadir.

evader, evasor.

evaluate, to, valuar, tasar.

evaluation, avalúo.

even number, número par.

ex dock, puesto en el muelle, franco en el muelle.

exceed, to, exceder.

excess-profit tax, impuesto sobre exceso de utilidades.

exchange, (*n.*) cambio, bolsa; (*v.*) cambiar.

— **adjustment,** ajuste sobre operaciones de cambio.

— **at par,** cambio a la par.

— **control,** control de cambios.

— **devaluation,** pérdida por conversión de moneda o por devaluación de moneda extranjera.

— **discount,** pérdida por conversión de moneda.

— **earnings,** ganancias por conversión de moneda.

— **margin,** margen de cambio.

— **permit,** permiso, autorización de cambio.

— **premium,** beneficio de cambio.

— **rate,** tipo de cambio.

— **value,** valor en cambio.

exchange-control board, junta de control de cambios.

exchequer bonds, bonos de la tesorería.

excise tax, impuesto sobre ventas.

exclusive, exclusivo, reservado.

— rights, derechos exclusivos.

— territory, territorio, mercado reservado.

execute a contract, to, firmar un contrato.

executed trust, fideicomiso formalizado.

executive, ejecutivo, funcionario.

— committee, comité ejecutivo.

— session, sesión ejecutiva.

executor, albacea.

exempt (*a.*) exento, libre; (*v.*) eximir.

exemption, exención, franquicia.

exogenous change, alteración económica debida a factores no económicos.

expand, to, aumentar, inflar.

expanded data, datos inflados.

expansion of capacity, expansión del poder productivo.

expectancy, life, probabilidad de vida.

expectation of proceeds, rendimiento esperado.

expectations, previsiones.

expected normal, normal, nivel previsto (normal).

expendable, gastable, desechable.

expenditure, gasto.

— control, control de gastos.

— estimates, cálculos de gastos.

—, government, gastos públicos.

expenses, gastos.

—, collection, gastos de cobranza.

—, development, gastos de expansión.

—, operating, gastos de operación.

—, shipping, gastos de embarque.

—, traveling, gastos de viaje.

expert accountant, experto en contabilidad.

expiration, vencimiento.

export, (*n.*) exportación; (*v.*) exportar.

— bond, fianza de exportación.

— bounty, subsidio para la exportación.

— declaration, declaración de exportación.

— drive, campaña en favor de la exportación.

— duty, derechos de exportación.

— **license,** licencia de exportación.

— **manager,** gerente de exportación.

— **permit,** permiso de exportación.

— **price,** precio de exportación.

— **quota,** cuota de exportación.

— **subsidies,** subsidios para la exportación.

— **surplus,** excedentes exportables.

— **trade,** comercio exterior (de exportación).

expropriate, to, expropiar, confiscar.

extend, to, extender.

extension, ampliación.

external, externo.

— **accounts,** cuentas de operaciones en el extranjero.

— **debt,** deuda exterior.

— **flow,** corriente externa.

— **imbalance,** desequilibrio de la balanza de pagos.

— **trade,** comercio exterior.

— **variance,** variancia externa.

extraordinary expenses, gastos extraordinarios.

F

face amount (face value), valor nominal.

facilities, instalaciones.

factor, factor, agente.

—, **balancing,** factor de compensación.

— **cost,** costo de factores.

— **income,** ingreso de los factores de producción.

factor's lien, gravamen de factor.

factory, fábrica, planta industrial.

— **overhead,** gastos de fábrica.

— **price,** precio de fábrica.

fail, to, quebrar, fallar, fracasar.

failure, quiebra, omisión.

fair, justo, equitativo.

— **cash value,** valor justo del mercado.

— **employment practices legislation,** leyes sobre sistemas justos de empleo.

— **market value,** valor justo del mercado.

— **price,** precio justo.

— **return,** beneficio justo.

— **value,** valor o precio justo.

Fair Deal, programa económico del Presidente Truman.

fall, (*n.*) caída, baja; (*v.*) caer.

— **due, to,** vencer.

— **in prices,** baja de precios.

— **of currency,** devaluación de la moneda.

false return, declaración (de impuestos) falsa.

family, familia.

— **allowance,** pensión, compensación familiar.

— **benefits,** subvención familiar.

— **expenses,** gastos familiares.

— **income,** ingreso familiar.

— **living expenditures,** gastos de mantenimiento de la familia.

— **partnership,** sociedad familiar.

far-reaching, de gran alcance.

farm operator, productor agrícola.

fe-sible, viable.

featherbedding, empleo de personal innecesario debido a las exigencias de los trabajadores.

federal, federal.

— **bills,** efectos financieros.

— **funds,** fondos federales.

— **income tax,** impuesto federal sobre ingresos.

fiduciary, fiduciario.

file, (*n.*) archivo, fichero; (*v.*) archivar, registrar, presentar.

final balance, saldo final.

finance, finanzas, financiar.

— **bills,** efectos financieros.

— **charges,** gastos financieros.

— **company,** sociedad financiera.

— **law,** legislación financiera.

financial, financiero.

— **assets,** activos financieros.

— **expedients,** expedientes financieros.

— **incentive,** estímulo financiero.

— **liability,** responsabilidad económica.

— **management,** dirección financiera.

— **period,** ejercicio financiero.

— **position,** situación financiera.

— **statement,** estado, balance financiero.

— **stringency,** situación financiera difícil.

— **year,** ejercicio, año económico.

financing, financiamiento, financiación.

findings, resultados de una encuesta o investigación.

fine, (*n.*) multa; (*v.*) multar.

finished products, productos acabados, terminados.

finite multiplier, multiplicador finito.

firm, firma, casa, firme.

— **name,** razón social.

— **prices,** precios firmes.

— **signature,** firma social.

first, primero.

— **lien,** primer gravamen o hipoteca.

— **mortgage,** primera hipoteca.

— **of exchange,** primera de cambio.

fiscal, fiscal.

— **burden,** carga fiscal.

— **domicile,** domicilio fiscal.

— **information service,** servicio de información en materia fiscal.

— **measures,** medidas fiscales.

— **period,** período contable, fiscal.

— **policy,** política fiscal.

— **year,** ejercicio, año fiscal.

fixed, fijo, determinado.

— **assets,** activo fijo.

— **capital,** activo fijo.

— **debt,** deuda consolidada.

— **duties,** derechos fijos.

— **interest bearing debentures,** obligaciones de interés fijo.

— **investment,** inversión de renta fija.

— **liabilities,** pasivo fijo.

— **rate of exchange,** tipo de cambio fijo.

— **tangible assets,** activo fijo tangible.

— **term,** plazo fijo.

fixed-income securities, valores de renta fija.

flat market, mercado flojo.

flat rate, tasa uniforme.

flight of capital, huída de capitales.

floating, flotante.

— **assets,** capital, activo flotante.

— **debentures,** obligaciones no consolidadas.

— **debt,** deuda flotante.

— **liabilities,** pasivo circulante.

— **policy,** póliza abierta.

floor price, precio mínimo.

F.O.B., *véase* **free on board.**

foodstuffs, productos alimenticios.

foot (ft), pie (0.3048 m).

force prices down, to, hacer bajar los precios.

forced, forzado, forzoso.

— **frugality,** frugalidad forzada.

— **sale,** venta forzosa.

— **saving,** ahorro forzado.

forecast, producer's, pronóstico de los productores.

foreign, extranjero.

— **bill,** letra sobre el exterior.

— **currency,** divisas, moneda extranjera.

— **debt,** deuda exterior, en el extranjero.

— **exchange,** divisas, cambio exterior.

— **grant,** subvención extranjera.

— **investment,** inversión extranjera.

— **securities,** valores extranjeros.

— **tax credit,** deducción por impuestos pagados en el extranjero.

— **trade,** comercio exterior.

foreign-exchange assets, activo en divisas.

foreign-exchange permit, permiso para operar con divisas.

foreseen, previsto.

foresight, previsión.

forge, to, falsificar.

forgery, falsificación.

form, forma, formulario.

forwarding agent, agente, expedidor aduanal.

foul bill of lading, conocimiento de embarque con reservas.

found business, to, establecer un negocio.

founder of a trust, fundador de un fideicomiso.

founder's shares, acciones de fundador.

founding stockholders, socios fundadores.

fractional shares, cupones de acción.

frame, to, formar, forjar.

franchise, franquicia, privilegio, patente, concesión de patente.

fraud, fraude, estafa.

free, libre, gratuito.

— **alongside,** libre al costado del vapor.

— **and clear,** libre de gravamen.

— **choice,** libre elección.

— **competition,** libre competencia.

— **enterprise,** libertad de empresa, iniciativa privada.

— **market,** mercado libre.

— **of charges,** libre de cargos.

— **on board, (F.O.B.),** libre a bordo, franco a bordo.

— **port,** puerto libre.

— **trade area,** zona de cambio libre.

freeze a credit, to, suspender un crédito.

freight collect, flete por cobrar.

freight prepaid, flete pagado.

frequency curve, curva de frecuencia.

frictional unemployment, desocupación debida a resistencias.

fringe benefits, prestaciones, beneficios adicionales al sueldo.

full, completo, total.

— **bill of lading,** conocimiento de embarque con responsabilidad completa del transportador.

— **employment,** empleo total.

— **endorsement,** endoso completo, a la orden.

— **payment,** pago total.

— **settlement,** liquidación, finiquito.

fully-paid shares, acciones cubiertas, exhibidas.

function, (*n.*) función; (*v.*) funcionar.

—, **consumption,** función consumo.

—, **demand,** función demanda.

fund, fondo.

—, **contingent,** fondo de contingencia, para contingencias.

—, **imprest,** fondo fijo (de trabajo).

—, **industrial insurance,** fondo para accidentes industriales.

—, **insurance,** fondo de seguro propio.

—, **pensión,** fondo de pensión.

—, **preferred stock sinking,** fondo de amortización de acciones preferentes.

—, **redemption,** fondo de redención o amortización.

—, **renewal,** fondo de reposición.

—, **reserve,** fondo de reserva.

—, **rotary,** fondo revolvente.

—, **sinking,** fondo de amortización.

—, **strike,** fondo de huelga.

—, **superannuation,** fondo de pensiones de vejez.

—, **trust,** fondo en o de fideicomiso.

fundable, consolidable.

funded, consolidado.

— **debt,** deuda consolidada.

— **liabilities,** pasivo fijo.

— **trust,** fideicomiso con depósito de fondos.

funding operation, operación de consolidación.

funds, fondos, dinero.

—, **public,** fondos públicos.

—, **working,** fondos de habilitación.

furnish money, to, financiar, refaccionar.

furniture and fixtures, mobiliario y equipo.

futures, futuros.

— **market,** mercado de futuros.

G

gain sharing, participación de utilidades.

gainful, lucrativo, ganancioso, provechoso.

— **activity,** actividad lucrativa.

— **employment,** ocupación lucrativa, provechosa.

gallon (gal), galón (E.U.: 3.785 l.) (Inglaterra: 4.546 l.).

gap, diferencia, brecha, déficit.

general, general.

— **acceptance,** aceptación sin reservas.

— **accounts,** cuentas generales.

— **agent,** agente, apoderado general.

— **average,** avería gruesa o común, promedio general.

— **expenses,** gastos generales.

— **meeting,** reunión general (de accionistas).

— **mortgage,** hipoteca colectiva.

— **partnership,** sociedad colectiva.

— **population movement,** movimiento general de la población.

— **rate,** impuesto general, uniforme.

— **strike,** huelga general.

generation life tables, tablas de mortalidad de generaciones.

gentlemen's agreement, pacto de caballeros.

genuine, genuino, legítimo.

geographic stratification, estratificación geográfica.

gift tax, impuesto sobre donaciones.

glut, superabundancia, exceso.

going concern, empresa en funcionamiento.

gold, oro.

— **coin and bullion,** oro acuñado y en barras.

— **payments,** pagos en oro.

— **point,** punto oro.

— **prices,** precios oro.

— **ratio,** proporción de la moneda de oro en relación con la circulación.

— **reserve,** reservas de oro.

— **standard,** talón, patrón oro.

— **subsidy program,** programa de subsidio del oro (para su producción).

goods, bienes mercancías, productos.

— **and services,** bienes y servicios.

—, **capital,** bienes de capital.

—, **consumption,** bienes de consumo.

—, **durable,** bienes duraderos.

— **in process,** productos en elaboración.

— **in transit,** mercancías en tránsito.

— **partly processed,** productos semiacabados.

goodwill, traspaso de clientela, guantes, plusvalía.

government, gobierno.

— **account,** cuenta del gobierno.

— **agency,** oficina, dependencia del gobierno.

— **authorities,** entidades oficiales.

— **bank,** banco del estado.

— **bonds,** bonos, títulos del estado.

— **employees,** empleados públicos.

— **enterprise,** empresa estatal.

— **expenditures,** gastos públicos.

— **loans,** préstamos, créditos otorgados por el gobierno.

— **monopoly,** monopolio del estado.

— **revenues,** ingresos fiscales.

— **sinking funds,** fondos de reserva del gobierno.

grace period, período de gracia (para pagar una deuda).

grades, commercial, normas, calidades comerciales.

graft, soborno, peculado.

grain, grano (64.7999 miligramos).

gram (g), gramo.

grant, (*n.*) subvención, concesión; (*v.*) conceder.

— **a patent, to,** conceder una patente.

— **credit, to,** conceder crédito.

graphical-numerical method, método numérico gráfico.

graphs, gráficas.

gratuity, gratificación.

gross, en bruto, grueso, general.

— **average earnings,** promedio de ingresos brutos.

— **earnings,** utilidad bruta.

— **income,** ingresos brutos.

— **national product,** producto nacional bruto.

— **output,** producción bruta.

— **profit,** utilidad bruta.

— **saving,** ahorro bruto.

— **weight,** peso bruto.

grouping interval, intervalo de agrupamiento.

guarantee, garantía, garantizar.

guarantor, fiador.

guaranty, garantía, caución.

— **bond,** fianza.

— **company,** compañía de fianzas.

— **fund,** fondo de garantía.

guild, asociación, hermandad, gremio.

H

hand, on, disponible, en existencia.

handicap, obstáculo, desventaja.

harbor dues, derechos de puerto.

head, cabeza.

— **of family,** jefe de familia.

— **office,** oficina principal, central.

— **tax,** impuesto por persona, por cabeza, capitación.

headquarters, oficina central, casa matriz, cuartel general.

hectare (ha), hectárea (10,000 m²).

hectogram (hg), hectogramo.

hectoliter (hl), hectolitro.

hectometer (hm), hectómetro.

hedge, (n.) resguardo; (v.) ponerse a cubierto, cubrirse.

hedging, operaciones para entrega futura (operaciones para cubrirse).

heir, heredero.

highest bidder, el mejor postor.

hindrance, rémora, obstáculo.

hire purchase, compra a plazos, compra en abonos.

hire, to, dar empleo.

historical cost, costo inicial.

hoarding, acaparamiento.

holder, tenedor, portador, poseedor.

holding company, compañía principal, matriz, propietaria de acciones.

holdings, haberes, disponibilidades.

home, hogar, domicilio, residencia.

— **economics,** economía doméstica.

— **market,** mercado interior.

— **office,** oficina principal, matriz.

honest, honrado, probo.

hot money, dinero adquirido por medio de transacciones monetarias ilegales.

hourly earnings, ganacias por hora.

hourly wages, salarios por hora.

house port, puerto de matrícula.

housing authority, autoridad sobre casas habitación.

housing shortage, escasez de viviendas.

I

idle, ocioso, inactivo.

— **capital,** capital improductivo.

— **time,** tiempo perdido, ocioso.

idleness, ociosidad, desocupación.

illegal, ilegal.

— **interest,** usura, interés ilícito.

— **strike,** huelga no autorizada.

illiquidity, iliquidez.

imitation, imitación, falso.

immigrant remittances, fondos enviados a su país por inmigrantes.

immovables, bienes raíces, inmuebles.

impair, to, empeorar, detereorar.

impending changes, cambios inminentes.

implication, deducción.

implied agreement, contrato sobrentendido, implícito.

import, (*n.*) importación; (*v.*) importar.

— **declaration,** declaración de importación.

— **duty,** derechos de importación.

— **license,** licencia o permiso de importación.

— **permit,** permiso de importación.

— **quota,** cuota de importación.

— **restrictions,** restricciones a la importación.

— **tariff,** arancel de importación.

import-replacing production, producción destinada a reemplazar la importación.

imports, importaciones.

— **on government account,** importaciones del estado.

— **on private account,** importaciones privadas.

impose a tax, to, imponer un impuesto.

impost, impuesto, contribución.

impound, to, depositar, incautar.

imprest, adelanto, préstamo.

— **cash funds,** fondos para gastos menores.

improve, to, mejorar, perfeccionar.

improved real estate, predio edificado.

improvements, mejoras.

inability, incapacidad.

inadequacy, insuficiencia.

inalienable, inajenable, inalienable.

incentive, estímulo, aliciente.

— wage system, sistema de salario incentivo, de bonificación por aumento de producción.

inch (in.), pulgada (2.54 cm).

incidence, incidencia.

incidental, concomitante.

— expenses, gastos varios.

— powers, poderes concomitantes.

incidentals, gastos imprevistos.

income, ingreso.

— account, estado de ingresos.

— bracket, categoría de ingreso.

— class, categoría de ingreso.

— deposits, depósitos para gastos de consumo.

— elasticity, elasticidad de ingreso.

— estimates, cálculos de ingreso.

— from business, ingresos mercantiles.

— from shares, dividendos (de acciones).

—, gross, utilidad, ingreso bruto.

— in kind, ingreso en especie.

— items, elementos de ingreso.

— level, nivel de ingresos.

— liable to tax, ingreso gravable.

— motive, motivo gasto de consumo.

—, net, ingreso líquido, neto.

— statement, declaración de ingresos.

— tax, impuesto sobre ingresos.

—, taxable, ingreso gravable.

income-tax return, declaración de ingresos.

income-velocity of money, velocidad-ingreso del dinero.

incorporate, to, incorporar, constituir.

incorporated company, sociedad anómina.

incorporation papers, contrato de sociedad, escritura constitutiva.

increase, (n.) aumento; (v.) aumentar.

increased cost, aumento del costo.

increment, unearned, plusvalía.

indebted, obligado, adeudado.

indebtedness, adeudo, deuda.

indefeasible, irrevocable, inabrogable.

indemnity, indemnización.

— **agreement,** pacto de indemnización.

— **bond,** contrafianza.

— **insurance,** seguro de indemnización.

independent variables, variables independientes.

index, índice.

— **of comparative mortality,** índice de mortalidad comparativa.

— **of physical production,** índice de la producción física.

— **of unit cost,** índice de costo unitario.

—**, production,** índice de producción.

—**, unit value,** índice de valores unitarios.

indictment, denuncia.

indirect, indirecto.

— **claim,** demanda por daño emergente.

— **collection,** cobro, recaudación indirecta.

— **damages,** daños indirectos.

— **labor,** mano de obra indirecta.

— **tax,** impuesto indirecto.

individual, individual, personal, individuo.

— **income tax,** impuesto individual sobre ingresos personales.

— **investor,** inversionista individual.

— **schedule,** programa o plan personal, cédula personal.

— **tax-paying capacity,** capacidad contributiva individual.

indorsement, (véase **"endorsement"**).

inducement to invest, incentivo para invertir.

inductive method, método inductivo.

industrial, industrial.

— **accident,** accidente de trabajo.

— **arbitration,** arbitraje industrial.

— **disputes,** conflictos de trabajo.

— **division,** distribución de actividades económicas.

— **education,** enseñanza vocacional.

— **injuries,** accidentes de trabajo.

— **insurance,** seguro industrial.

— **partnership,** participación de utilidades (con los obreros).

— **planning,** planeación industrial.

— **relations,** relaciones obrero-patronales, relaciones laborales.

— **securities,** títulos industriales.

— **union,** gremio industrial.

industry, industria.

ineffectual, ineficaz.

inefficiency, ineficiencia.

inelastic, inelástico.

inequitable, injusto.

inequity, falta de equidad.

infant industry, industria naciente.

inflationary effect, efecto inflacionista.

inheritance tax, impuesto sobre herencias.

inland bill of lading, conocimiento de embarque por tierra.

inland freight, flete terrestre.

inner harbor, puerto interior.

input, insumo, inyección, compras.

—, current, insumo corriente.

input-output, insumo producto.

— **coefficient,** coeficiente insumo producto.

insolvency, insolvencia.

inspect, to, inspeccionar, revisar.

instability, inestabilidad.

installment plan, plan de ventas en abonos.

installment sales, ventas en abonos, a plazos.

instruct, to, dar instrucciones.

instrument, documento, escritura.

instrumental capital, capital instrumental.

insurable risks, riesgos asegurables.

insurance, seguro.

— **broker,** corredor, agente de seguros.

— **company,** compañía de seguros, aseguradora.

— **fund,** fondo para seguros.

— **policy,** póliza de seguro.

— **premium,** prima de seguro.

— **trust,** fideicomiso de seguro.

insure, to, asegurar, asegurarse.

insured, asegurado.

insurer, asegurador.

intangible assets, activo nominal, aparente.

intangibles, activo intangible.

intensive sampling, muestreo intensivo.

interact, to, reaccionar entre sí.

interblock variance, variancia interbloque.

inter-country comparisons, comparaciones entre países.

interest, interés, participación, rédito.

—, **compound,** interés compuesto.

— **cost,** cargo por pago de intereses.

— **rate,** tasa de interés.

interest-dividend, interés dividendo.

interest-free loan, empréstito sin interés.

interest-yielding assets, activo con rendimiento de intereses.

interim

— **balance sheet,** balance tentativo.

— **budget,** presupuesto provisional.

statement, estado, provisional, declaración provisional.

intermediary, intermediario.

intermittent demand, intermitencias en la demanda.

internal revenue, ingreso interior.

internal revenue tax, impuesto fiscal. Véase **excise tax.**

international, internacional.

— **tax agreements,** acuerdos fiscales internacionales.

interstate commerce, comercio interstatal.

intervene, to, intervenir.

invalidate, to, anular.

invalidity, invalidez, nulidad.

inventory, inventario.

—, **closing,** inventario final.

— **control,** control de existencias.

—, **opening,** inventario inicial.

—, **physical,** inventario físico.

— **records,** libro de almacén, de bodega.

— **turnover,** movimiento, rotación de existencias.

— **valuation,** valoración de las existencias.

—, **valued,** inventario valorado.

invest, to, invertir.

invested capital, capital aportado.

invested demand-schedule, curva de la demanda de inversión.

investment, inversión.

— **banking,** banco de inversiones.

— **company,** compañía inversionista.

— **goods,** bienes de inversión (en equipo).

—, **gross,** inversión bruta.

— **in kind,** inversión en especie.

— **multiplier,** multiplicador de inversión.

— **policy,** política de inversion.

investor, inversionista.

invisible trade, comercio invisible.

invoice, (*n.*) factura; (*v.*) facturar.

invoicing, facturación.

involuntary unemployment, desocupación involuntaria.

I.O.U., pagaré.

irredeemable bond, obligación no amortizable.

irregular dividend, dividendo ocasional.

irrevocable letter of credit, carta de crédito irrevocable.

issue, (*n.*) emisión de valores; (*v.*) emitir.

— **above par,** emisión sobre la par.

— **below par,** emisión bajo la par.

— **department,** departamento emisor.

— **price,** precio de emisión.

item, artículo, elemento, partida, renglón, concepto.

itemize, to, detallar.

itemized account, cuenta detallada.

J

job, (*n.*) obra, trabajo, corretaje; (*v.*) comprar y vender en calidad de corredor.

— **evaluation,** clasificación del trabajo por su calidad.

— **lot,** lote de mercancías, saldo.

jobber, intermediario, corredor.

jobbery, agiotaje (sobre fondos públicos).

John Bull, Inglaterra.

John Doe, fulano de tal.

joint, mancomunado, colectivo.

— **account,** cuenta mancomunada, en participación.

— **committee,** comisión mixta.

— **cost,** costos de producción común a dos o más productos.

— **creditors,** coacredores.

— **debtors,** codeudores, deudores mancomunados.

— **estate,** propiedad mancomunada.

— **heirs,** coherederos.

— **liability,** obligación mancomunada.

— **owner,** copropietario.

— **products,** productos simultáneos.

— **session,** sesión plenaria.

— **transactions,** transacciones comunes.

joint-stock company, sociedad en comandita (por acciones).

jointly, mancomunadamente.

journal, libro diario (de contabilidad).
— **entry,** asiento de diario.
junior partner, socio menor.

jurisdictional strike, huelga intergremial sobre jurisdicción.

K

keep, (*n.*) manutención, subsistencia; (*v.*) guardar, conservar.
—, **to earn one's,** ganarse la vida.
keeping, book, teneduría de libros.
key exports, exportaciones clave.
key industries, industrias clave.
kickback, pago que un empleado debe dar a su patrón

o jefe para poder conservar su empleo.
kilogram (kg), kilogramo.
kiloliter (kl), kilolitro.
kilometer (km), kilómetro.
kind, in, en especie.
kiting, circulación de cheques sin fondo.
knock-out price, precio muy rebajado.
know-how, destreza, habilidad, pericia, experiencia, conocimientos prácticos.

L

labor, (*n.*) trabajo, personal asalariado; (*v.*) trabajar.
— **agreement,** contrato colectivo de trabajo.
— **code,** ley de trabajo, derecho obrero.
— **court,** tribunal del trabajo.
— **dispute,** conflicto de trabajo.
— **federation,** federación de trabajadores.

— **force,** personal obrero.
— **groups,** grupos de trabajadores.
— **income,** ingreso del trabajo.
— **jurisdiction,** jurisdicción del trabajo.
— **laws,** derecho obrero.
— **market,** mercado de mano de obra.
— **relations,** relaciones obrero-patronales.

— **turnover,** número de obreros que reemplazan a los que dejan el trabajo.

— **union,** gremio, sindicato obrero.

— **unit,** unidad de trabajo.

labor-saving devices, dispositivos o aparatos para ahorrar mano de obra.

laborer, trabajador, jornalero, peón.

lag, (n.) retraso; (v.) retrasarse.

land, tierra, terreno.

— **freight,** flete terrestre.

— **grant,** concesión, donación de tierras.

— **office,** oficina del catastro.

— **reform,** reforma agraria.

— **tax,** impuesto sobre terrenos, predial.

— **under lease,** terreno arrendado.

landholder, terrateniente.

landless, sin tierra.

landowner, terrateniente.

landslide, derrumbe, mayoría de votos abrumadora.

large sample, muestra grande.

large scale, en grande, en grande escala.

law, ley, derecho.

— **breaker,** infractor de la ley.

— **of diminishing returns,** ley del rendimiento decreciente.

lawsuit, litigio, acción judicial.

lawyer, abogado, licenciado.

lay-days, días de estadía, de demora (de un barco).

lay off, despido (de obreros), paro forzoso, retiro temporal de obreros.

lay out, to, proyectar.

leakage, merma.

lean year, año magro, pobre.

lease (n.) arrendamiento, arriendo; (v.) arrendar, alquilar.

ledger, libro mayor.

— **entry,** asiento en el mayor.

— **value,** valor en libros.

legacy tax, impuesto sobre sucesiones.

legal, legal, lícito.

— **entity,** persona moral.

— **interest,** interés al tipo legal.

— **reserve,** reserva legal.

— **strike,** huelga autorizada.

— **tender,** moneda de curso legal.

— **weight,** peso legal.

lend, to, prestar.

— **on collateral,** prestar con respaldo colateral.

— **on mortgage,** prestar sobre hipoteca.

letter, carta, letra.

— **of attorney,** carta poder.

— **of credit,** carta de crédito.

— **of guaranty,** carta de garantía.

— **of indemnity,** carta de indemnización.

level, nivel.

— **of monetary rewards,** nivel de remuneración monetaria.

— **out, to,** nivelar.

leveling off of the volume of export, estabilización del volumen de las exportaciones.

levy, (*n.*) impuesto, contribución; (*v.*) gravar, imponer.

— **taxes, to,** imponer contribuciones, impuestos.

liabilities, obligaciones, pasivo.

—, **actual,** pasivo real.

—, **assumed,** pasivo asumido.

—, **contingent,** pasivo contingente.

—, **current,** pasivo flotante.

—, **fixed,** pasivo fijo o consolidado.

—, **indirect,** pasivo indirecto o contingente.

—, **matured,** pasivo vencido.

— **reserve,** reserva de pasivo.

—, **secured,** pasivo garantizado.

—, **trade,** pasivo comercial.

—, **unsecured,** pasivo no garantizado.

liability, obligación, pasivo, responsabilidad.

— **accounts,** cuentas de pasivo.

— **for endorsement,** responsabilidad por endoso o aval.

—, **joint,** pasivo mancomunado.

—, **personal,** pasivo u obligación personal.

—, **unlimited,** responsabilidad ilimitada.

liable for tax, gravable, sujeto a impuesto.

liable to, susceptible de.

license, licencia, patente.

— **fees,** derechos de licencia.

licensee, concesionario, permisionario.

lien, gravamen, embargo precautorio.

— **creditor,** acreedor embargador.

life, vida, duración, vigencia.

— **annuity,** anualidad, pensión vitalicia.

— **expectancy,** duración media de vida.

— **insurance policy,** póliza de seguro de vida.

— **interest,** usufructo vitalicio.

— **member,** socio vitalicio.

— **of a patent,** plazo, vigencia de una patente.

likeproduct, producto similar.

limited, limitado.

— **company,** compañía, sociedad de responsabilidad limitada.

— **liability,** responsabilidad limitada.

— **partnership,** sociedad limitada.

line of business, género de actividad comercial.

line sampling, muestreo de líneas.

lineal estimation, estimación lineal.

liquid, líquido, disponible, realizable.

— **assets,** activo circulante, líquido.

— **market,** mercado activo.

— **resources,** recursos líquidos, realizables.

liquidate, to, liquidar, pagar.

liquidated, liquidado, pagado.

— **damages,** daños liquidados.

— **debt,** deuda liquidada.

liquidation statement, estado de liquidación.

liquidator, liquidador, ajustador.

liquidity, liquidez, disponibilidad.

— **preference,** preferencia por la liquidez.

— **premium,** prima de liquidez.

—, **scale of,** escala de liquidez.

—, **standard of,** patrón de liquidez.

list price, precio de lista, de catálogo.

listed securities, valores bursátiles.

liter (l.), litro.

living, vivo, activo.

— **level,** nivel de vida.

— **trust,** fideicomiso activo.

loan, préstamo, empréstito.

— **account,** cuenta de préstamo.

— **for consumption,** préstamo de consumo.

— **for use,** préstamo de uso.

— **on debentures,** préstamo en obligaciones.

— **refunded (redeemed) (repaid),** préstamo amortizado, reembolsado.

local, local, regional.

— **customs,** costumbres de la plaza.

— **draft,** letra de plaza.

— **taxes,** impuestos locales.

lock out, cierre, dejar sin trabajo a los obreros para obligarlos a pactar.

logistic population, población logística.

long-period, de período largo.

— **employment,** ocupación a largo plazo.

long-term, a largo plazo.

loss, pérdida.

—**, gross,** pérdida bruta.

—**, net,** pérdida neta.

lot, partida, lote.

low-income group, grupo de personas de ingresos reducidos.

low-interest loans, présta-

mos a bajo interés.

low-yield bond, bono de rendimiento bajo.

lump-sum contract, contrato a precio alzado, en cantidad global.

luxury goods, artículos de lujo, bienes suntuarios.

M

machinery and equipment, maquinaria y equipo.

macro-economic comparison, comparación macroeconómica.

main estimates, cálculos básicos.

maintenance, conservación.

majority interest, interés mayoritario.

make available, to, poner a disposición.

makeshift, improvisado, provisional.

man-hours, hora mano de obra.

manage, to, administrar, dirigir.

managed economy, economía dirigida.

management, dirección, gerencia, administración.

— **of funds,** administración, manejo de fondos.

— **shares,** acciones de fundador o de administración.

manager, administrador, gerente, director.

managing partner, socio gerente o administrador.

manifest, manifiesto (de carga de un barco).

manpower, mano de obra.

manual workers, obreros, jornaleros.

manufacturer's price, precio de fábrica.

margin, margen.

— **of preference,** margen de preferencia.

— **of profits,** margen de utilidades.

marginal, marginal.

— **cost,** costo marginal.

— **disutility,** desutilidad marginal.

— **efficiency of capital,** eficacia marginal del capital.

— **expenditures,** gastos marginales.

— **factor cost,** costo marginal de los factores.

— **proceeds,** importe marginal de ventas.

— **propensity to consume,** propensión marginal a consumir.

— **supplies,** abastecimientos marginales.

— **unit,** unidad marginal.

— **user cost,** costo marginal de uso.

marine, marítimo, marino.

— **risk,** riesgo marítimo.

— **underwriters,** aseguradores contra riesgos marítimos.

maritime contract, contrato marítimo.

mark-down, reducción de precios.

mark-up, (*n.*) diferencia entre el costo total y el precio de venta, sobreprecio; (*v.*) aumentar el precio.

marked price, precio fijado, marcado.

marker's price, precio de fábrica.

market, mercado, plaza, bolsa.

—**, at,** a precio de plaza, de mercado.

—**, buyers,** mercado del comprador.

— **expectations,** previsiones del mercado.

—**, futures,** mercado a término, de futuros.

— **method,** método de precios del mercado.

—**, open,** mercado libre.

— **price,** precio corriente, del mercado.

— **rate of interest,** tasa de interés del mercado.

— **trends,** tendencias del mercado.

— **value,** valor en plaza, de mercado.

marketability, negociabilidad.

marketable, negociable, comerciable, vendible.

— **title,** título negociable.

marketing, técnica comercial, mercadotecnia.

mart, mercado.

Mary Doe, fulana de tal.

mass production, producción en masa, en serie.

matched samples, muestras concordantes.

materials, raw, materias primas.

mathematical demography, demografía matemática.

mathematical expectation of gain, previsión matemática de ganancias.

mature, to, vencer, cumplirse el plazo.

maturity, vencimiento, plazo.

— date, fecha de vencimiento.

— of bills, vencimiento de las letras.

— value, valor al vencimiento.

maximize, to, elevar al máximo.

maximum likelihood estimator, estimador del máximo de verosimilitud.

maximum likelihood method, método del máximo de verosimilitud.

mean age at death, edad media al morir.

mean size of family, tamaño medio de las familias.

mean, weighted, media ponderada.

mean-square error, error cuadrático medio.

means of communication, medios de comunicación.

measure, (*n.*) medida, recurso; (*v.*) medir.

medium-size family, familia de tamaño medio.

meet conditions, to, sujetarse a condiciones.

meet specifications, to, cumplir con las especificaciones.

meet the price, to, aceptar el precio.

meeting, reunión, conferencia, asamblea.

member of the firm, socio de la firma.

mercantile, mercantil, comercial.

— law, derecho mercantil.

merchandise, mercancía, mercadería.

merchandising profit, utilidad comercial.

merchant, comerciante.

— guild, asociación de comerciantes (época medioeval).

merge, to, combinar, fusionar, unir.

merger, incorporación, fusión, unión.

meter (m), metro.

method, método, procedimiento.

—, market price, método del precio del mercado.

— of selected points, método de los puntos elegidos.

—, price of last purchase, método del precio de la última compra.

—, retail, método del menudeo, de la venta al por menor.

middleman, intermediario, revendedor.

migration of labor, migración de mano de obra.

migration statistics, estadísticas de migración.

mile (mi), milla (terrestre: 1.609 km) (marítima: 1.852 km).

milligram (mg), miligramo.

milliliter (ml), mililitro.

millimeter (mm), milímetro.

minimize, to, reducir al mínimo.

minimum wage, salario mínimo.

minor, menor de edad.

minority, minoría.

— interest, interés minoritario.

— stockholders, accionistas de la minoría.

mint, (*n.*) casa de moneda; (*v.*) acuñar moneda.

minutes, actas, minutas.

misappropriation, malversación de fondos.

miscalculation, error de cálculo.

miscellaneous commodities, mercancías varias.

miscellaneous expenses, gastos varios.

miserliness, avaricia.

misleading, engañoso.

mixed model, modelo mixto.

mixed sampling, muestreo mixto.

mobility of labor, movilidad del trabajo.

moderate price, precio módico, razonable.

monetary, monetario.

— gold stock, existencias de oro acuñado.

— stabilization loan, empréstito para estabilizar la moneda.

— supply, disponibilidad monetaria, oferta monetaria.

money, dinero.

— allotment, asignación de fondos.

— at call, disponibilidades a la vista.

— balance, saldo en efectivo.

— capital, capital monetario.

— income, ingreso monetario.

— market rate, tasa del mercado monetario.

— order, giro postal o bancario.

— supply, disponibilidades monetarias, medio circulante.

— wage, salario monetario.

money-commodity, dinero mercancía.

moneylender, prestamista.

monoculture, monocultivo.

monopolist, monopolista, acaparador.

monopolize, to, monopolizar, acaparar.

monopoly, monopolio, acaparamiento.

— **prices,** precios de monopolio.

monopsony, monopolio del comprador.

moratory, moratorio.

mortality, mortalidad.

mortgage, (*n*.) hipoteca; (*v*.) hipotecar.

— **bank,** banco hipotecario.

— **certificate,** cédula hipotecaria.

— **debenture,** obligación hipotecaria.

mortgagee, acreedor hipotecario.

mortgagor (mortgager), deudor hipotecario.

most-efficient estimator, estimador de eficiencia máxima.

most favored-nation clause, cláusula de la nación más favorecida.

most-powerful test, prueba más poderosa.

motive, motivo.

—, **business,** motivo negocios.

— **income,** motivo gasto de consumo.

—, **precautionary,** motivo precaución.

—, **speculative,** motivo especulativo.

—, **transactions,** motivo transacción.

movable property, bienes muebles.

movements in birth, movimientos de natalidad.

movements, capital, movimientos de capital.

multilateral, multilateral.

— **agreement,** convenio multilateral.

— **arbitrage scheme,** sistema de arbitraje multilateral.

— **trade,** comercio multilateral.

multiple, múltiple.

— **exchange rates,** tasas múltiples.

— **rate of exchange,** tasa de cambio múltiple.

— **stratification,** estratificación múltiple.

— **taxation,** imposición múltiple.

multiple-phase process, proceso multifásico.

multiplier, multiplicador.

mutual assistance, ayuda mutua.

mutual fund, fondo mutualista.

mutually exclusive classes, clases mutuamente excluyentes.

N

national debt, deuda nacional.

national product, producto nacional.

nationalize, to, nacionalizar.

native produce, productos domésticos nacionales.

natural resources, recursos naturales.

negligence, negligencia, imprudencia.

negotiable, negociable, transmisible.

— **instruments,** instrumentos negociables.

— **paper,** efectos negociables.

— **securities,** valores transmisibles.

negotiate, to, tratar, negociar.

net, neto, líquido.

— **assets,** activo neto.

— **book value,** valor neto en libros.

— **business income,** ingreso mercantil neto.

— **capital formation,** formación neta de capital.

— **expenditures,** gastos netos.

— **foreign investment account,** cuentas de inversiones extranjeras netas.

— **income,** ingreso neto.

— **investment,** inversión neta.

— **migration,** saldo migratorio.

— **output,** producción neta.

— **price,** precio neto.

— **reproduction rate,** tasa neta de reproducción.

— **savings,** ahorro neto.

— **value added,** valor agregado neto.

— **weight,** peso neto.

— **worth,** activo neto.

non-par-value stock, acciones sin valor nominal.

nominal, nominal.

— **capital,** capital autorizado.

— **damages,** indemnización nominal o insignificante.

— **gold par,** paridad nominal del oro.

— **partner,** socio nominal.

nominate, to, nombrar, designar.

nonacceptance, falta de aceptación.

nonamortizable loan, empréstito no amortizable.

nonassenting stockholders, accionistas disidentes.

nonassessable stock, acciones no gravables.

noncash economy, economía no monetaria.

noncommercial, no comercial.

nondiscriminatory assistance, ayuda no selectiva.

nondiscriminatory import restrictions, restricciones no selectivas a la importación.

nondutiable, franco de impuestos.

nonessential goods, bienes no esenciales, no necesarios.

nonexpendable equipment, equipo permanente.

nonfactor services, servicios no correspondientes a los factores de producción.

nonfamily group housing, vivienda del grupo no familiar.

noninterest-bearing, que no devenga interés.

nonmarket product, producto no comercializado.

nonmember
— **bank,** banco no respaldado, fuera de la cámara de compensación.
— **broker,** corredor no reconocido en la bolsa de valores.

nonmonetary goods, bienes no monetarios.

nonnegotiable, no negociable, intransferible.

nonnull hypothesis, hipótesis de no nulidad.

nonoperating income, ingresos no provenientes de la operación.

non-par-value-stock, acciones sin valor nominal.

nonparametric tests, pruebas no paramétricas.

nonparametric tolerance limits, límites de tolerancia no paramétricas.

nonprofit-making corporation, asociación no lucrativa.

nonrandom sample, muestra no aleatoria.

nonrecurring expense, gastos ocasionales.

nonrenewable, no renovable, no prorrogable.

nonresident, no residente.

nonrestrictive endorsement, endoso sin restricciones.

nonstock corporation, sociedad sin acciones.

nontaxable, no gravable, exento de impuestos.

nonvoting stock, acciones sin derecho a voto.

non-static, dinámico.

non-wage-earners, quienes no ganan salarios.

non-wage-goods, artículos para asalariados.

normal, normal.

— **income,** ingreso normal.

— **residence,** residencia permanente.

— **tax,** impuesto normal o básico.

notary's office, notaría.

note, pagaré, nota, documento.

—, **credit,** nota de crédito.

—, **debit,** nota de cargo.

—, **promissory,** pagaré.

notes payable, documentos por pagar.

notes receivable, documentos por cobrar.

notify, to, notificar, avisar, participar.

null and void, nulo y sin valor.

nullify, to, anular, invalidar.

O

obligated capital, capital suscrito.

obligation, obligación, título.

obsolescence, caída en desuso.

occupation tax, impuesto de empleo o de profesión.

occupational, relativo a la profesión u oficio.

— **accident,** accidente de trabajo.

— **death rate,** tasa de mortalidad por profesiones.

— **disease,** enfermedad profesional.

— **hazard,** riesgo profesional.

— **injury,** lesión, accidente de trabajo.

ocean freight, flete marítimo.

odd-lot broker, corredor que compra y vende acciones en lotes menores de cien.

offer, (*n.*) oferta; (*v.*) ofrecer.

offered price, precio de oferta.

office, oficina, despacho, agencia.

officer, oficial, funcionario.

official, oficial.

offset, (*n.*) cancelación, compensación, contrapartida; (*v.*) neutralizar, oponer.

— **dumping, to,** neutralizar el "dumping".

offsetting factors, factores compensatorios.

old-age benefits, prestaciones por vejez.

old-age pension, pensión por vejez.

oligopoly, monopolio parcial, monopolio de unos pocos.

omission, omisión.

omit, to, omitir, suprimir.

on account, a cuenta.

on consignment, en consignación.

on demand, a la vista, a la presentación.

one-crop economy, monocultura.

one-price, precio único.

one-sided test, prueba unilateral.

open-country population, población rural.

open-door policy, política de puerta abierta.

open-market operations, operaciones en el mercado abierto.

open-market rate of exchange, tipo de cambio del mercado libre.

open population, población abierta.

opening balance, saldo de apertura.

opening price, precio de apertura.

operating

— **capital,** capital de explotación.

— **characteristic function,** función característica operante.

— **company,** empresa de explotación.

— **costs,** costos de explotación.

— **deficit,** pérdida, déficit de explotación.

— **expenditures,** gastos de explotación, ordinarios.

— **income,** ingresos de explotación, ordinarios.

— **loss,** pérdida de explotación.

— **surplus,** excedente de explotación.

operational budget, presupuesto de explotación.

optimum, óptimo.

— **number,** número óptimo.

— **population,** población óptima.

— **sum,** la suma más favorable.

order, (n.) orden, pedido, decreto; (v.) ordenar, encargar.

— **of business,** orden del día, temario.

— **of the day,** orden del día.

—, **to place an,** hacer un pedido.

ordinary, normal, corriente.

— **budget,** presupuesto ordinario.

— **meeting,** junta ordinaria.

— **member,** miembro titular.

— **session,** sesión o junta ordinaria.

— **term,** período ordinario.

original, original.

— **acquisition,** adquisición original.

— **allotment,** asignación inicial.

— **capital,** capital inicial.

— **cost,** costo inicial.

— **entry,** asiento en el diario, primera entrada.

— **stock,** acciones primitivas.

ounce (avoirdupois)(oz avdp.), onza (28.350 gramos).

ounce (fluid) (fl oz), onza (E.U.: 29.573 ml) (Inglaterra: 28.412 ml).

out of date, caducado.

outbid, to, mejorar, pujar, ofrecer más que otros compradores.

outflow, salida, exportación.

outgo, erogaciones, gastos.

outgoing, saliente.

outlays, gastos (de operación).

outlet, salida.

output, producto, producción.

— **factor,** factor de producción.

—, **gross,** producción bruta.

—, **net,** producción neta.

outsell, to, competir en ventas, vender más barato.

outstanding,

— **capital,** capital suscrito.

— **contracts,** contratos en curso.

— **debts,** deudas existentes.

— **money,** moneda en circulación.

— **securities,** acciones o títulos emitidos.

— **stock,** capital suscrito, acciones en manos del público.

outward bound, con destino al extranjero.

over-all authorization, autorización global.

over-all financial results, resultados financieros globales.

overcharge, to, cobrar demasiado, sobrecargar.

overcredit, to, abonar de más.

overdebit, to, debitar de más.

overdraft, sobregiro, giro en descubierto.

overdraw, to, sobregirar, girar en descubierto.

overdue, vencido, atrasado.

overexposure, sobreexposición.

overhead, sobrecarga, gastos indirectos.

— **expenses,** gastos generales o indirectos.

— **charges,** gastos generales.

overinvestment, inversión excesiva, sobreinversión.

overissue, emisión excesiva.

overlap, (n.) traslapación; (v.) traslapar.

overload, sobrecarga, sobrecargar.

overloading, sobrecarga.

overlook, to, pasar por alto.

overpayment, pago excesivo.

overproduction, superproducción.

overstate, to, exagerar, abultar.

overstocking, almacenamiento excesivo.

oversupply, superabundancia de la oferta.

overtime, tiempo extra, horas suplementarias de trabajo.

overvalue, to, valuar en exceso.

owner, dueño, propietario.

ownership, propiedad, pertenencia.

P

pact, acuerdo, pacto, convenio.

packing list, especificaciones de embalaje.

paid in full, totalmente pagado, liquidado.

paid-in surplus, excedente de capital.

paid-up capital, capital exhibido, pagado.

paid-up stock, acciones cubiertas.

paper money, papel moneda, (también **paper currency**).

par, par, paridad.

—, above, sobre par.

—, below, bajo par.

— items, efectos cobrables sin comisión.

— of exchange, cambio a la par, paridad cambiaria.

— value, valor a la par, de paridad.

parameter point, punto parámetro.

parameter space, espacio parámetro.

parcel post, envío de paquetes por correo.

pare down expenditures, to, reducir los gastos.

parent company, compañía matriz, principal o propietaria.

parent house, casa matriz, compañía controladora.

parity income ratio, razón de paridad de ingresos.

parity price, precio de paridad.

part settlement of claims, ajuste parcial de reclamaciones.

partial, parcial.

— acceptance, aceptación condicionada.

— loss, pérdida parcial.

— replacement, reposición parcial.

participating stock, acciones preferentes participantes.

particular average, pérdida parcial.

particulars, conceptos, detalles.

partner, socio, asociado.

partnership, sociedades, asociación.

— **agreement,** pacto socia, lcontrato de asociación.

— **articles,** escrituras de sociedad.

— **assets,** bienes sociales.

— **at will,** asociación sin plazo fijo de duración.

— **contract,** contrato social, de asociación.

— **debt,** deudas sociales.

— **property,** bienes sociales.

pass, to, pasar, aprobar, transmitir.

— **book,** libreta de banco, de depósitos.

— **the dividend, to,** omitir el pago de dividendos.

passive, pasivo.

— **assets,** activo intangible.

— **bond,** bono sin interés.

— **debt,** deuda sin interés.

— **liabilities,** pasivo fijo.

— **trust,** fideicomiso pasivo.

passport, pasaporte.

patent, (*n.*) patente; (*v.*) patentar.

— **and trademark office,** oficina de patentes y marcas.

— **application,** solicitud de patente.

— **law,** ley, derecho de patentes.

— **license,** licencia de patente.

— **office,** oficina de patentes.

— **pending,** patente pendiente, en tramitación.

— **royalty,** regalía por uso de patente.

patented process, proceso patentado.

patrimony, patrimonio.

pattern of trade, situación comercial.

pawn, prenda, dar en prenda, empeñar.

pay, to, pagar, remunerar.

— **back,** restituir.

— **by installments,** pagar en abonos, a plazos.

— **in full,** pagar por completo, pagar la totalidad.

— **off a mortgage,** redimir una hipoteca.

— **on account,** pagar a cuenta.

— **to the order of,** pagar a la orden de.

— **warrant,** autorización, orden de pago.

pay-as-you-go policy, pago de impuestos a medida que el contribuyente recibe sus ingresos.

payable, pagadero, por pagar.

— **at sight,** pagadero a la vista, a la presentación.

— **on demand,** pagadero a la presentación.

— **to bearer,** pagadero al portador.

— **to order,** pagadero a la orden.

payables and receivables, sumas por pagar y por cobrar.

payee, beneficiario, tenedor, portador.

payer, pagador.

paying agent, agente pagador.

paymaster, pagador.

— **list,** nómina de pagos.

payment, pago, paga.

— **in full,** pago total.

— **in kind,** pago en especie.

— **refused,** pago rehusado, negado.

payroll, nómina de pagos, lista de raya.

— **tax,** impuesto sobre sueldos.

peak, punto máximo.

peculation, peculado, desfalco.

pegged price, precio de estabilización.

penalty clause, cláusula penal (en un contrato).

penalties, multas, sanciones, recargos.

pension, pensión, jubilación.

— **deferred,** pago diferido de pensión.

— **fund,** fondo de pensión.

— **rights,** derechos de pensión o jubilación.

— **trust,** fideicomiso de pensiones.

per capita, por cabeza, por persona.

per cent, por ciento.

per diem, por día, diario.

percentage, por ciento, porcentaje.

— **of completion method,** método de porcentaje de terminación.

— **of profit,** porcentaje de utilidades.

perfunctorily, superficialmente.

peril point clause, cláusula de punto crítico.

period, período.

periodic migrations, migraciones periódicas.

permanent, permanente.

— **assets,** capital fijo.

— **debt,** deuda permanente.

— **equipment,** equipo fijo.

— **fixtures,** instalaciones fijas.

— **home,** lugar de residencia permanente.

— **migration,** migración permanente.

— **partial disability,** incapacidad parcial permanente.

— **total disability,** incapacidad absoluta permanente.

permeated with, permeado de.

permissive use, uso pasivo.

permit (n.) licencia, permiso; (v.) permitir.

permittee, tenedor de permiso de patente.

perpetual, perpetuo.

— **annuity,** anualidad perpetua.

— **bond,** bono sin vencimiento.

— **loan,** empréstito no amortizable, perpetuo.

— **trust,** fideicomiso perpetuo.

person having custody of titles, persona depositaria de títulos.

personal, personal, particular.

— **bond,** fianza particular, personal.

— **deduction,** deducción individual.

— **disability,** incapacidad individual.

— **estate,** bienes muebles.

— **exemption,** exención personal.

— **finance company,** sociedad para préstamos menores.

— **income,** ingreso personal.

— **income tax,** impuesto sobre ingresos personales.

— **liability,** responsabilidad personal de accionistas.

— **property,** bienes muebles.

— **tax,** impuesto personal.

personnel manager, jefe de personal.

petition in bankruptcy, petición de quiebra.

physical, físico.

— **assets,** valores materiales.

— **disability,** incapacidad física.

— **impossibility,** imposibilidad material.

pick-up in demand, aumento de demanda.

picket line, cordón de huelguistas.

piecework, trabajo a destajo.

pilferage, hurto, sisa.

pilot sample, muestra piloto, de orientación.

pilot study, estudic de orientación.

pint (liquid) (pt), pinta (E.U.: 0.473 l.) (Inglaterra: 0.568 l.).

place of business, local del negocio.

planned economy, economía dirigida.

planning board, junta de planificación, planeación.

planning, industrial, planeación industrial.

plant capacity, capacidad de producción.

pledge, prenda, garantía, colateral, empeñar.

— **loan,** préstamo prendario.

pledgeable, pignorable.

plenary meeting, sesión plenaria.

plow back profits, to, reinvertir las utilidades.

plural-voting stock, acciones de voto plural.

plurality, pluralidad.

policy, política, práctica, póliza.

— **of non-discriminatory import restrictions,** política de restricciones no selectivas a la importación.

— **of restraint,** política de austeridad.

policyholder, tenedor de póliza.

politics, política (social).

poll, (*n.*) votación, sondeo de la opinión pública; (*v.*) votar.

— **tax,** impuesto por cabeza, por persona.

pool, (*n.*) combinación, convenio, fusión; (*v.*) combinar.

pooling of errors, combinación de errores.

poor laws, leyes de beneficencia.

population, población.

— **center,** centro de población.

— **displacement,** desplazamiento de población.

— **policy,** política demográfica.

— **pyramid,** pirámide de población.

— **recorded,** población registrada.

— **trend,** tendencia demográfica.

port, puerto.

— **authorities,** autoridades portuarias.

— **duties,** derechos portuarios.

— **of call,** puerto de escala.

— **of delivery,** puerto terminal.

— **of distress,** puerto de emergencia.

— **of entry,** puerto fiscal, de entrada.

— **of shipment,** puerto de embarque.

portfolio, lista de valores que se poseen, cartera.

position, posición, situación económica.

possess, to, poseer, tener.

possessor, poseedor.

possessory title, título posesorio.

postal savings bank, caja postal de ahorros.

postdated, posfechado.

posted price, precio impuesto, tarifa oficial.

postpone, to, aplazar, posponer.

post-quota surplus, excedente de cuota.

postwar, postguerra.

potential density, densidad potencial.

pound (avdp.), libra (453.59 gramos).

poverty, pobreza, indigencia.

power, autoridad, poder.

— in gross, poder sin interés del apoderado.

— of appointment, facultad de nombrar.

— of attorney, carta poder, para transar.

practicability, posibilidad de ejecución.

practicable, viable, factible.

precautionary motive, motivo precaución.

predial servitude, servidumbre predial.

prefer, to, dar preferencia.

preference, preferencia, prioridad.

— bond, bono privilegiado.

— share, acción privilegiada.

— stock, acciones privilegiadas.

preferential, preferente, privilegiado.

— price, precio preferencial.

— tariff, tarifa preferencial.

— trading systems, sistemas de comercio preferencial.

preferred, preferido.

— creditor, acreedor privilegiado.

— debt, deuda de prioridad, privilegiada.

— dividend, dividendo sobre acciones privilegiadas.

— lien, gravamen preferente.

— procedure, procedimiento preferente.

— stock, acciones preferidas, privilegiadas.

— stockholder, accionista preferido.

premises, local, establecimiento.

premium dollars, dólares vendidos con bonificación.

— prepayment, pago anticipado.

prescribe, to, prescribir.

prescribed error, error prescrito.

prescribed range of error, amplitud de error prescrito.

prescriptive owner, propietario por prescripción.

present, to, presentar, dar.

— for payment, presentar al pago.

present worth, valor actual.

presumptive method, método de probabilidad.

pretax earnings, utilidades antes de los impuestos.

prevailing price, precio dominante, en vigor.

preventive rights, derechos precautorios.

previous endorsement, endoso anterior.

price, (*n.*) precio; (*v.*) poner precio.

— **adjustment,** ajuste de precios.

—, **agreed,** precio convenido.

— **as provided in the contract,** precio según contrato.

—, **average,** precio medio.

—, **cash,** precio al contado.

—, **ceiling,** precio tope.

— **control,** control de precios.

—, **cost,** precio de costo.

— **freeze,** congelación de precios.

— **index,** índice de precios.

— **inflation,** inflación de precios.

— **leader,** precio piloto, determinante.

— **level,** nivel de precios.

— **list,** lista de precios, tarifa.

— **margin,** margen de utilidad.

— **pattern,** comportamiento de los precios.

—, **prospective,** precio probable.

—, **purchase,** precio de compra.

— **regulation,** reglamentación de precios.

— **resistance,** resistencia contra los altos precios.

—, **sales,** precio de venta.

— **steadiness,** estabilidad de precios.

— **strengthening,** estabilización de precios.

— **subsidy,** subsidio de precios.

— **support policy,** política de sostenimiento de precios.

prices, precios.

—, **floor,** precios mínimos.

—, **monopoly,** precios de monopolio.

—, **retail,** precios al menudeo.

primary, primario.

— **allotment,** asignación inicial.

— **commodity,** producto primario.

— **liability,** responsabilidad directa.

— **materials,** materias primas.

— **producing countries,** países productores de materias primas.

— **products,** productos primarios.

— **rights,** derechos primarios.

— **wants,** artículos de primera necesidad.

prime cost, costo primo.

prime rate, tasa preferencial.

principle, principio.

print money, to, imprimir dinero.

prior preferred stock, acciones preferidas superiores.

priority bond, bono privilegiado.

private, particular, privado.

— **bank,** banco particular, sin incorporar.

— **consumption,** consumo privado.

— **enterprise,** empresa privada, iniciativa privada.

— **foreign investments,** inversiones privadas extranjeras.

— **income,** ingreso particular privado.

— **property,** propiedad privada, bienes particulares.

— **rights,** derechos individuales, particulares.

— **sale,** venta directa.

— **trust,** fideicomiso particular, privado.

privilege, privilegio, concesión.

priviledged debt, deuda privilegiada, preferida.

probability, probabilidad.

— **integral,** integral de probabilidad.

— **of surviving,** probabilidad de sobrevivencia.

— **rate,** tasa de probabilidad.

— **ratio test,** prueba de la razón de la probabilidad.

— **surface,** superficie de probabilidad.

probable duration of life at birth, duración probable de vida al nacer.

probable income, ingreso probable.

proceeds, productos.

process, (*n.*) elaboración; (*v.*) elaborar.

processing

— **error,** error de elaboración.

— **of products,** elaboración de productos.

— **tax,** impuesto por elaboración.

produce, (*n.*) producto, producción; (*v.*) producir.

producer's

— **forecasts,** pronósticos de los productos.

— **goods,** bienes de producción.

— **price,** precio de fábrica.

product, producto.

— **flow,** corriente de productos.

production, producción.

— **account,** cuenta de producción.

— **cost,** costo de producción.

— **factors,** factores de producción.

— **index,** índice de producción.

— **profit,** beneficio, utilidades de producción.

— **tax,** impuesto sobre producción.

productive investment, inversión productiva.

productivity, productividad.

profit, (*n.*) utilidad, ganancia, lucro; (*v.*) lucrar.

— **and loss,** pérdidas y ganancias.

— **and loss statement,** estado de pérdidas y ganancias.

— **motive,** motivo lucro, con fines de lucro.

— **sharing,** reparto, participación de utilidades.

— **tax,** impuesto sobre utilidades.

profit-earning capacity, capacidad lucrativa.

profit-seeking, con finalidades lucrativas.

profitable, provechoso, beneficioso, productivo.

profiteer, acaparador, agiotista.

profits, utilidades.

—, **accumulated,** utilidades acumuladas.

—, **anticipated,** utilidades anticipadas.

—, **book,** utilidades aparentes, en libros, según libros.

—, **capitalized,** utilidades capitalizadas.

—, **casual,** utilidades extraordinarias.

—, **contingent,** utilidades contingentes.

—, **deferred,** utilidades por realizar.

—, **departmental,** utilidades departamentales.

—, **distributed,** utilidades pagadas, distribuidas.

—, **distributive,** utilidades repartibles.

—, **extraordinary,** utilidades extraordinarias.

—, **gross,** utilidades brutas.

—, **inflated,** utilidades infladas.

—, **net,** utilidades netas.

—, **paper,** utilidades no realizadas.

—, **realized,** utilidades realizadas.

— **tax,** impuesto sobre beneficios, sobre utilidades.

—, **taxable,** utilidades gravables.

—, **undistributed,** utilidades no pagadas, no repartidas.

programming, elaboración de programas, programación.

progress payments, pagos escalonados.

progressive surtax, sobretasa, sobreimpuesto progresivo.

prohibitive prices, precios prohibitivos.

promissory note, nota de pago, pagaré.

promote, to, fomentar, promover.

promotion, promoción, fomento.

—, trade, fomento del comercio.

proof, prueba, comprobación.

propensity, propensión.

— to consume, propensión a consumir.

— to hoard, propensión a atesorar.

— to invest, propensión a invertir.

— to save, propensión a ahorrar.

property, bienes, haberes, propiedad.

— damage, daños materiales.

— dividend, dividendo de bienes, en especie.

— rights, derechos de propiedad.

— tax, impuesto sobre bienes.

property-increment tax, impuesto de plusvalía.

proportional, proporcional.

— rates, tasas proporcionales.

— sampling, muestreo proporcional.

— tax, impuesto proporcional.

pro-rata, en proporción, a prorrata.

— repartition of assets, repartición proporcional del activo.

prorate, to, prorratear.

prorogation, prórroga.

prospecting of foreign markets, exploración de mercados extranjeros.

prospective, probable, esperado, anticipado.

— damages, daños anticipados.

— price, precio probable.

— yield, rendimiento probable.

protective duty, derechos proteccionistas.

protective tariff, tarifa proteccionista.

protest, protesto, protestar.

protest charges, gastos de protesto.

protested bill, letra protestada.

protestee, protestado.

protester, protestador.

provision, disposición (legal).

provisional mean, promedio provisional.

proxy, poder, carta poder.

—, by, por poder.

— holder, poderhabiente, apoderado.

public, público.

160

— **accountant,** contador público.

— **auction,** subasta pública.

— **body,** organismo público.

— **opinion polls,** encuestas, sondeos de la opinión pública.

— **policy,** política pública.

— **property,** bienes de dominio público, fiscales.

— **revenue,** renta fiscal, ingresos públicos.

— **sale,** subasta con aviso anticipado.

— **treasury,** erario, tesorería.

— **trust,** fideicomiso público.

— **undertaking,** empresa pública.

— **utilities,** empresas de servicio público.

— **welfare,** bienestar público.

— **works,** obras públicas.

public-service

— **commission,** comisión de servicio público

— **corporation,** empresa o compañía de servicio público.

— **utilities,** servicios públicos.

public-utility securities, títulos de empresas de servicio público.

punitive action, medida represiva.

purchase, (*n.*) compra; (*v.*) comprar.

— **price,** precio de compra.

— **tax,** impuesto sobre ventas.

purchasing power, poder adquisitivo.

put in a bid, to, licitar.

Q

qualifications, requisitos, salvedades, calificaciones, títulos.

qualified, limitado, condicionado, calificado.

— **acceptance,** aceptación limitada o condicionada.

— **endorsement,** endoso condicionado.

— **monopoly,** monopolio limitado.

— **owner,** tenedor de interés limitado.

qualifying shares, acciones habilitantes.

qualitative, cualitativo.

quality goods, mercancías de calidad.

quantitative, cuantitativo.

— **indeterminacy,** indeterminación cuantitativa.

— **probabilities,** probabilidades cuantitativas.

quantum of exports, volumen físico de las exportaciones.

quart (liquid) (qt.), cuarto de galón (E.U.: 0.946 l.) (Inglaterra: 1.13 l.).

quarter, trimestre.

quarterly, trimestralmente.

quasi-rent, cuasi-renta.

quay, muelle, embarcadero.

quick assets, activo disponible.

quota, cuota.

—, **export,** cuota de exportación.

— **system,** sistema de cuotas.

quotation, cotización.

R

railroad transportation, transporte ferroviario.

raise, to, alzar, levantar, cultivar.

— **a check,** aumentar el importe de un cheque.

— **a loan,** conseguir un préstamo, un empréstito.

— **funds,** conseguir fondos.

— **money,** conseguir fondos.

raising factor, factor de aumento.

random, aleatorio, fortuito, sin proyectar.

—, **at,** al azar.

— **impulse process,** proceso de impulso aleatorio.

— **order,** orden aleatorio.

— **sample,** muestra al azar.

— **sampling error,** error del muestro aleatorio.

— **start,** comienzo aleatorio.

randomization, aleatorización.

randomized blocks, bloques aleatorizados.

range of values, escala de valores.

ratable, valuable, tasable.

rate, (n.) tasa, tipo, coeficiente, tarifa; (v.) tasar, valuar.

— **base,** valuación base para tarifas.

— **book,** libro de tarifas.

—, **effective interest,** tasa real del interés.

— **of exchange,** tipo de cambio.

— **of freight,** tarifa de flete.

— **of growth,** tasa de crecimiento.

— **of increase,** tasa de aumento, de crecimiento.

— **of interest,** tasa de interés.

— **of issue,** curso de emisión.

— **of return,** tasa de rendimiento.

— **regulation,** control de tarifas.

rate of exchange chart, gráfica de la razón de cambio.

rated concern, empresa clasificada por agencias de crédito.

rating, tasación, valor asignado, clasificación de una empresa según su posición financiera.

ratio, razón, coeficiente, índice.

— **estimate,** estimación de la razón.

— **of solvency,** índice de solvencia.

ration, to, racionar.

— **out, licenses,** restringir las licencias.

rationing, racionamiento.

— **of credits,** racionamiento, restricción de créditos.

raw materials, materias primas.

— **turnover,** movimiento de materias primas.

reacceptance, reaceptación.

readjusting entry, contrapartida.

readjustment of currencies, reajuste monetario.

ready cash, fondos disponibles.

ready money, efectivo, fondos disponibles.

real, real, verdadero.

— **assets,** bienes inmuebles.

— **burden,** carga real.

— **income,** ingreso real.

— **price,** precio real.

— **product measure,** medida del producto real.

— **property,** bienes raíces, inmuebles.

— **rate of exchange,** tipo de cambio real.

— **securities,** garantías hipotecarias.

— **wages,** salarios reales.

real-estate, bienes raíces.

— **bond,** bono inmobiliario.

— **broker,** corredor de bienes raíces.

— **tax,** impuesto sobre inmuebles, predial.

realization value, valor en liquidación.

realized income, ingresos vencidos.

realized results, resultados obtenidos.

realtor, corredor de bienes raíces.

realty, bienes raíces.

reappraisal, reavalúo.

reappraise, to, revaluar.

reappraisement, revaluación.

re-arrangement, disposición nueva.

re-arranging, reclasificación.

rebate, rebaja, bonificación, descuento.

receipt, recibo, talón.

— in full, finiquito.

—, on, al recibo de.

receipts, recibos, percepciones, ingresos, entradas.

— journal, libro diario de entradas.

—, tax, ingresos fiscales.

receivables, cuentas por cobrar.

— ledger, libro mayor de cuentas por cobrar.

receive, to, recibir, percibir.

received payment, recibí.

receiver, receptor, liquidador, síndico.

receiving teller, recibidor, cajero recibidor.

recession, depresión.

recharter, to, refletar.

recipient, recibidor, beneficiario.

reciprocal, recíproco.

— contract, contrato bilateral, recíproco.

— exemption, exención recíproca.

— trade agreements, tratados comerciales recíprocos.

reciprocity principle, principio de reciprocidad.

reckoning, cálculo, ajuste de cuentas.

reclamation, recuperación, aprovechamiento de tierras.

recognize a debt, to, admitir una deuda.

reconsignment, cambio de destinatario de una mercancía.

record (*n.*) registro, acta; (*v.*) registrar.

recording on a cash basis, método de la contabilidad de caja.

recording secretary, secretario de actas.

records, registros, archivos.

recount, (*n.*) recuento; (*v.*) recontar.

recoup, to, recuperar.

recover, to, recuperar, cobrar, recobrar.

recoverable accounts, cuentas recobrables.

recovery, recuperación, cobranza.

— value, valor de recuperación.

recurring, recurrente, que se repite.

— samples, muestras que se repiten.

red tape, papeleo, formulismo.

redate, to, poner fecha nueva.

redeem, to, redimir, rescatar, amortizar.

redeemable, redimible, rescatable, amortizable.

redeemed, redimido, rescatado, amortizado.

redemption, rescate.

— allowance, amortización autorizada.

— fund, fondo de rescate, caja de amortización.

— of the public debt, amortización de la deuda pública.

— price, precio de rescate.

rediscount, (*n.*) redescuento; (*v.*) redescontar.

reduce, to, reducir.

reduced output, producción disminuida, reducida.

reduced rate, tarifa reducida.

reducing-balance method of depreciation, método de saldo decreciente.

reducing-charge method, método de depreciación con cargos decrecientes.

redundancy, sobrante, redundancia.

redundant stock, existencias sobrantes, redundantes.

refund, (*n.*) devolución, reembolso; (*v.*) devolver, reembolsar.

refundable tax, impuesto reembolsable.

refunding bonds, bonos de reintegración.

refusal, negativa, rechazo.

refuse, (*n.*) desecho; (*v.*) rehusar, rechazar.

— acceptance, to, negar o rehusar la aceptación.

— payment, to, rehusar el pago.

regional cartel, monopolio regional.

register, (*n.*) registro; (*v.*) registrar.

— a trademark, to, registrar una marca de fábrica.

— a vessel, to, abanderar un barco.

registered, registrado, titulado.

— bond, bono nominativo.

— capital, capital social.

— check, cheque de administración.

— debentures, obligaciones nominativas.

— securities, títulos nominativos, registrados.

— shares, acciones nominativas, registradas.

— stock, acciones nominativas, registradas.

— trademark, marca registrada.

registration, registro.

— fees, derechos de registro.

— record, acta de registro.

registry, registro.

— of vital statistics, registro demográfico.

regular, corriente, ordinario.

— **budget,** presupuesto ordinario.

— **mail,** correo ordinario.

— **meeting,** asamblea o junta ordinaria.

— **member,** miembro titular.

— **session,** sesión o junta ordinaria.

— **term,** período ordinario.

— **unbiased critical region,** región crítica sin preferencia.

regulation, reglamento, reglamentación.

reimbursable advances, anticipos reembolsables.

reimburse, to, reembolsar, reintegrar.

reimbursement credit, crédito de reembolso.

reinstate, to, restablecer reincorporar.

reject, to, rechazar, rehusar.

relationship, relación.

relax credit, to, facilitar el crédito.

relaxation, relajamiento.

— **of restrictions,** disminución de restricciones.

re-lease, to, rearrendar.

release, (*n.*) descargo, finiquito; (*v.*) descargar, librar.

relet, to, recontratar.

reliability, confiabilidad.

reliable, confiable, fidedigno.

— **source,** de buena fuente.

relief, asistencia, socorro, beneficencia.

—, **on,** viviendo de la ayuda del estado, de la beneficencia.

— **works,** obras para reducir el desempleo.

relieve shortages, to, remediar la escasez.

remake, to, rehacer.

remedy, remedio, recurso.

remission, remesa, remisión.

— **of a tax,** reducción o cancelación de un impuesto.

remit, to, remitir, enviar, situar.

remittance, envío, remesa.

remittances, giros de fondos.

remunerate, to, remunerar.

remunerative price, buen precio.

render, to, rendir, hacer.

— **an account,** rendir una cuenta, pasar facturas.

renegotiate, to, reajustar, renegociar.

renew, to, renovar, prorrogar.

renewal, renovación, prórroga.

—, **capital,** reinversión de capital.

rent, (*n.*) alquiler, arriendo; (*v.*) alquilar, arrendar.

— **factors,** factores de renta.

rental, arriendo, alquiler.

— **value,** valor por concepto de alquiler.

repay, to, reembolsar.

repayment, reembolso.

repeal, to, derogar (una ley).

replacement, reposición, re-emplazo.

— **cost,** costo de reposición (de equipo).

report, (*n.*) informe, relación; (*v.*) informar.

represent, to, representar.

representative, representante, representativo.

reproduction cost, costo de reposición, de reproducción.

request, solicitud, demanda.

requirements, requisitos, estipulaciones.

requisites, requisitos.

rescind, to, rescindir.

research, (*n.*) investigación; (*v.*) investigar.

reservations and safe-guards, reservas y garantías.

reserve, (*n.*) reserva; (*v.*) reservar.

— **above normal,** reserva superior a lo normal, excedente.

—, **allowances,** reserva para bonificaciones.

—, **benefit-fund,** reserva para auxilios a empleados.

—, **contingent,** reserva de contingencia.

— **for bad debts,** reserva para deudas incobrables.

— **for depletion,** reserva para agotamiento.

— **for discounts,** reserva para descuentos.

— **for taxes,** reserva para impuestos.

— **for wear, tear, obsoles-cence and inadequacy,** reserva para desgaste depreciación, desuso e insuficiencia.

— **fund,** fondo de reserva.

—, **hidden,** reserva oculta.

—, **industrial-accident-fund,** reserva para accidentes industriales.

—, **pension-fund,** reserva para pensiones.

— **price,** precio mínimo fijado en una subasta.

—, **profit-sharing,** reserva para participación de utilidades.

— **ratio,** relación de reserva.

—, **relief-fund,** reserva para auxilios a empleados.

—, **renewals and replace-ments,** reserva para renovación y reposición.

—, **sinking-fund,** reserva para amortización.

—, **uncollectable accounts,** reserva para cuentas incobrables.

residence, residencia, domicilio.

resident, habitante, vecino, residente.

— **company,** compañía que funciona en el lugar o estado de incorporación.

residual balance, saldo residual.

residual product, subproducto.

resign, to, renunciar, dimitir.

resolution, acuerdo, decisión.

resolve, to, acordar, resolver.

resources, medios, recursos.

responsible, responsable, solvente.

rest, resta, resto, saldo, diferencia.

resting point, punto de reposo.

restoration of stock, restauración de las existencias.

restrain, to, restringir.

restricted, restringido, reservado.

— **bond,** bono no transferible.

— **imports,** importaciones restrigidas, controladas.

— **market,** mercado reservado.

— **randomization,** aleatorización restringida.

— **sampling,** muestreo restringido.

retail, (*n.*) menudeo, detalle; (*v.*) vender al por menor.

— **merchandise,** mercancías de menudeo, al por menor.

— **method,** método de precio de menudeo, de precio al por menor.

— **price,** precio de menudeo.

— **sales tax,** impuesto sobre las ventas de menudeo, sobre ventas al por menor.

— **trade,** comercio por menor o de menudeo.

retailer, vendedor al por menor.

retained earning, beneficios no distribuidos.

retaliatory tariff, impuestos de represalia.

retirement, retiro, jubilación.

— **age,** edad de jubilación.

— **annuity,** pensión de retiro.

— **fund,** fondo de pensión.

retransfer, retransmisión.

retroactive payment, pago de sueldos atrasados.

return, producto, rendimiento, beneficio.

— **of capital,** rendimiento del capital.

returns, producto, ingreso, utilidades.

returnable advances, anticipos reembolsables.

revaluation, revaluación, revalorización (de la moneda).

revenue, ingresos, renta, rendimiento.

— **authorities,** fisco, administración fiscal.

— **bond,** bono del estado.

— **duties,** derechos fiscales.

— **laws,** leyes fiscales.

— **purposes, for,** con fines fiscales.

— **stamp,** timbre fiscal.

— **tariff,** arancel fiscal.

reversal, inversión, cambio, revocación.

reverse coding, codificación inversa.

revise, to, enmendar, codificar.

revision, modificación, revisión.

revolving credit, crédito renovable.

revolving fund, fondo renovable.

reward, gratificación, premio.

right, derecho, título, privilegio.

— **of property,** derecho de dominio.

— **to strike,** derecho de huelga.

rise, alza, aumento.

rising prices, precios al alza.

risk function, función del riesgo.

road tax, impuesto para conservación de caminos.

rollback of prices, baja de precios.

rotation of crops, rotación de cultivos.

rotation of stocks, rotación de existencias.

rough, basto, en bruto, aproximado.

— **draft,** borrador.

— **estimate,** presupuesto aproximado.

— **sorting,** clasificación aproximada.

roundabout process, proceso indirecto.

rounded age, edad redondeada.

routine, rutina, rutinario.

routine list, lista ordinaria.

royalty, regalía, derechos de patente.

rule, regla, reglamento.

ruling price, precio en vigor.

run low, to, agotarse.

runaway inflation, inflación violenta, desmedida.

running expenses, gastos ordinarios (de operación).

rural credits, créditos agrícolas.

rural non-farm population, población rural no agrícola.

rush order, pedido urgente.

S

sabotage, sabotaje, sabotear.

sacrifice, sacrificio, sacrificar.

sacrifice, at, con pérdida.

safe, caja de seguridad, seguro, a salvo.

safe deposit box, caja de seguridad (de un banco).

safeguard, (*n.*) resguardo, garantía; (*v.*) proteger.

sagging market, mercado flojo.

salability, vendibilidad.

salable, vendible.

salary, sueldo, salario.

sale, venta.

— **note,** nota de venta.

— **on credit,** venta a crédito.

— **price,** precio de venta.

— **proceeds,** productos de las ventas.

sales, ventas.

— **consultant,** asesor sobre métodos de ventas.

— **control,** control de ventas.

— **department,** gerencia o departamento de ventas.

— **discount,** descuento por pronto pago.

— **force,** personal de ventas.

— **manager,** gerente de ventas.

— **policy,** plan, sistema de ventas.

— **ratio,** índice de ventas.

— **tax,** impuesto sobre ventas.

— **terms,** condiciones de venta.

salvage, salvamento, recuperación, salvar, recobrar.

— **agreement,** contrato de salvamento.

— **charges,** cargos de salvamento.

sample, muestra.

— **line,** línea de muestreo.

— **point,** punto de muestreo.

— **size,** tamaño de la muestra.

— **space,** espacio de muestreo.

— **statistics,** estadística de la muestra.

— **survey,** encuesta por muestra.

sampler, muestreador.

sampling, muestreo.

— **bias,** bias del muestreo.

— **inspection,** inspeccción por muestreo.

— **procedure,** procedimiento de muestreo.

— **tolerance,** tolerancia del muestreo.

— **variability,** variabilidad en el muestreo.

— **variance,** variancia del muestreo.

— **with replacement,** muestreo con reposición.

save, to, ahorrar.

savings, ahorros.

— and loan association, sociedad de ahorro y préstamos.

— bank, banco, caja de ahorros.

— bonds, títulos de ahorro.

— deposits, depósitos de ahorro.

scale, escala.

— of apportionment, escala de repartición.

— of global progression, escala de progresión global.

— of liquidity, escala de liquidez.

— of progression, escala de progresión.

— of wages, escala de sueldos, escalafón.

scarcely populated area, área escasamente poblada.

scatter

— chart, gráfica de dispersión.

— coefficient, coeficiente de dispersión.

— diagram, diagrama de dispersión.

schedule, tabla, curva, plan, programa, horario.

—, demand, tabla, curva de demanda.

— of concessions, lista de concesiones.

— of duties, arancel.

— of par values, tabla de valores a la par.

—, supply, tabla de oferta.

scheduled costs, costos proyectados.

scheme, proyecto, plan.

scrap, material de desecho.

scrape equipment, to, retirar equipo.

screening, depuración.

scrip, vale, certificado.

sea carrier, empresa naviera.

sea letter, permiso de navegación.

sealed bids, propuestas selladas.

season, temporada, estación.

seasonal, estacional, de estación.

— demand, demanda de temporada.

— goods, artículos de temporada.

— migration, migración estacional.

— unemployment, desempleo estacional.

— variation, variación estacional.

— worker, trabajador de temporada.

seasonally adjusted, reajustado según la estación.

second of exchange, segunda de cambio.

secondhand goods, artículos de segunda mano, usados.

secular

— **fluctuations,** fluctuaciones, variaciones a largo plazo.

— **stagnation,** baja actividad económica durante un largo período.

— **trend,** curso, tendencia a largo plazo.

secured, asegurado, garantizado.

— **bond,** bono hipotecario.

— **claim,** reclamación garantizada.

— **loan,** préstamo garantizado.

securities, valores, títulos.

— **market,** mercado bursátil, de valores.

security, títulos, garantía.

— **holders,** tenedores de títulos.

— **holdings,** títulos en portafolio.

— **ratings,** clasificación de valores.

— **register,** registro de valores.

seizure, embargo.

selection, selección.

— **with arbitrary, probability,** selección con probabilidad arbitraria.

— **with equal probability,** selección con igual probabilidad.

— **with probability proportional to size,** selección con probabilidad proporcional al tamaño.

self-adjusting, que se ajusta en forma automática.

self-consumption, autoconsumo.

self-correcting sample, muestra de autocorrección.

self-financed, autorefaccionado, autofinanciado.

self-liquidating, autoliquidable, autoamortizable.

self-sufficiency, independencia económica.

self-sustaining reaction, reacción automantenida.

self-weighted sample, muestra autoponderada.

sell, to, vender.

— **at auction,** rematar, vender en subasta.

— **at loss,** vender con pérdida.

— **at profit,** vender con ganancia.

— **at the closing market,** vender a precio de cierre.

— **at the opening market,** vender a precio de apertura.

— **forward,** vender para entrega futura.

— **off,** liquidar.

— **on consignment,** vender en consignación.

— **short,** vender en descubierto (previendo una baja en el mercado).

— **up,** liquidar.

seller, vendedor.

seller's market, mercado del vendedor.

selling price, precio de venta.

semifinished, semielaborado, semiacabado.

— **product,** producto semielaboradao.

semimanufactured products, productos semielaborados.

semi-skilled, semiespecializado.

seniority, antigüedad.

sequence of economic events, serie de fenómenos económicos.

sequential sample, muestra sucesiva.

serial, seriado, de serie.

— **bonds,** bonos de vencimiento en serie, escalonado.

— **number,** número de serie.

series, serie.

service, charge, cargo por servicios.

servitude, servidumbre.

set, to

— **a price,** fijar un precio.

— **aside,** reservar, apartar.

set of bills of lading, juego de conocimientos de embarque.

set price, precio fijado.

setback, retroceso, contratiempo.

settle to, ajustar, arreglar, resolver.

— **a bill,** cancelar una factura.

— **a strike,** solucionar una huelga.

— **up,** pagar.

settlement, arreglo, ajuste, liquidación.

—, **full,** saldo final, finiquito.

settling day, día de liquidación.

severance pay, pago de despido, indemnización de despido.

share, (*n.*) acción, participación; (*v.*) participar.

— **capital,** capital en acciones.

— **certificate,** certificado de acciones.

— **premium,** prima de emisión.

— **without par value,** acción sin valor nominal.

shareholder, accionista.

shares, acciones.

shift, movimiento, cambio, desplazamiento.

ship broker, corredor, agente marítimo.

shipment, embarque, envío.

— **on consignment,** embarque a consignación.

shipper, embarcador, remitente.

shipper's export declaration, declaración de exportación.

shipping, embarque, envío; barcos, naviero.

— **advice,** aviso de embarque.

— **agent,** agente embarcador, despachador.

— **business,** empresa de transportes marítimos.

— **charges,** gastos de embarque.

— **company,** empresa naviera.

— **conference,** asociación de empresas de transporte marítimo.

— **documents,** documentos de embarque.

— **expenses,** gastos de embarque, de expedición.

— **instructions,** instrucciones de embarque.

— **marks,** marcas de embarque.

— **port,** puerto de embarque.

— **ring,** asociación de empresas de transporte marítimo.

— **weight,** peso de embarque.

ships' papers, documentación del barco.

ship's passport, certificado de navegación.

shop, (*n.*) taller, fábrica; (*v.*) buscar el precio más bajo.

shopping center, centro, zona comercial.

short, corto, escaso.

— **delivery,** entrega incompleta.

— **supply,** escasez.

short-date, a corto plazo.

short-period, de períodos cortos.

short-term-bond, bono a corto plazo.

short-time bill, letra a corto plazo.

shortage, escasez.

shorthand, taquigrafía.

shortsightedness, imprevisión.

shrinkage, merma, contracción, pérdida de peso o volumen de una mercancía.

sight

—**, at,** a la vista, a la presentación.

— **bill,** letra a la vista.

— **draft,** giro, letra a la vista.

— **letter of credit,** carta de crédito a la vista.

signature, firma.

significance level, nivel de significación.

significance test, prueba de significación.

significant quantities, cantidades importantes.

simple cost functions, funciones de costo simple.

simple sample, muestra simple.

sinecure, canonjía, sinecura.

single

— **crop country,** país de monocultivo.

— **entry,** partida simple.

— **sample,** muestreo en una etapa.

— **tax,** impuesto único.

single-price policy, sistema de precios únicos.

sinking fund, fondo de amortización.

sit-down strike, huelga de brazos caídos.

site, sitio, lugar.

skilled trade, oficio calificado.

skilled worker, obrero calificado.

slack season, temporada de depresión.

slashed prices, precios reducidos.

sliding scale, escala móvil.

slow, lento.

— **assets,** activo solamente disponible a largo plazo.

slow-moving goods, mercancías de salida lenta o difícil.

slum clearance, supresión de barrios bajos malsanos.

slump, depresión económica.

smuggle, to, contrabandear.

social, social.

— **capillarity,** capilaridad social.

— **demography,** demografía social.

security, previsión social, seguridad social.

social-security tax, impuesto de seguro social.

soft currency, moneda de valor inestable.

soil conservation, conservación de suelos, de tierras.

sold, vendido.

solvency, solvencia.

source, origen, proveniencia.

— **country,** país de origen.

specific income categories, categorías de ingresos específicos.

speculate, to, especular.

speculative motive, motivo especulativo.

speculator, especulador, agiotista.

speed up, aumento de producción por hora o por día.

spending power, poder para gastar.

split shares, to, dividir las acciones.

spoil, to, deteriorar, descomponerse.

spoiled check, cheque inutilizado.

sponsor, patrocinador, fiador.

spot
— **contract,** contrato al contado.
— **delivery,** entrega inmediata.
— **exchange,** cambio del día.
square foot (ft²), pie cuadrado (9.29 dm²).
square meter (m²), metro cuadrado (10.7639 ft²).
square mile (mi²), milla cuadrada (2.590 km²).
square yard (yd²) yarda cuadrada (0.836 m²).
— **price,** precio inmediato.
stability, estabilidad.
stabilization fund, fondo de establización.
stabilize, to, estabilizar.
stabilizer, fuerza estabilizadora.
stable, estable.
staff, miembros de la administración, personal.
stage, etapa.
— **of completion,** etapa de acabado.
stagnation, business, paralización de los negocios.
stale
— **B/L,** conocimiento de embarque tardío.
— **check,** cheque caducado.
— **debt,** deuda caducada.
stale-dated, de fecha atrasada.
stamp, (*n.*) timbre, sello; (*v.*) estampar, imprimir.

— **duties,** impuesto del timbre.
— **tax,** impuesto del timbre.
standard, norma, patrón.
— **accounts,** cuentas tipo.
— **classification,** clasificación uniforme.
— **costs,** costos tipo.
— **of liquidity,** patrón de liquidez.
— **of living,** nivel de vida.
— **port,** puerto de referencia.
— **practice,** sistema tipo.
— **ratio,** razón estándar, normal.
— **sample,** muestra tipo.
— **time,** hora oficial.
— **weight,** peso legal.
standards, international, normas internacionales.
standing charges, cargos permanentes.
standing costs, costos permanentes.
standpoint, punto de vista.
staple, materia prima, producto principal o básico.
— **commodities,** productos básicos.
— **industry,** industria de productos básicos.
starting point, punto de arranque.
state tax, impuesto estatal.
stated capital, capital declarado.

statement, declaración, relación, estado cuenta.

—, financial, estado financiero, balance general.

— ledger, mayor de estados mensuales (en bancos).

— of account, estado o extracto de cuenta.

— of affairs, estado financiero.

— of assets and liabilities, estado activo y pasivo, balance financiero.

— of condition, estado de situación.

— of financial position, balance general.

— of income, estado de ingresos.

—, operating, estado de resultados de operación.

—, profit and loss, estado de pérdidas y ganancias.

—, pro-forma, estado en proforma.

stationary population, pobblación estacionaria.

stationary process, proceso estacionario.

statism, economía dirigida, estatismo, control de la economía por el gobierno.

statistical, estadístico.

— inquiry, investigación estadística.

— map, cartograma.

— probability, probabilidad estadística.

statistics, estadística, datos estadísticos.

status, estado (civil o legal).

statute, estatuto, ley.

— of limitations, estatuto de limitaciones, de prescripción.

statutes, estatutos, escritura.

statutory, estatutario.

— bond, fianza legal.

— coefficients, coeficientes legales.

— provisions, disposiciones legales.

stay of collection, suspensión de pago.

steady market, mercado de poca fluctuación.

steady prices, precios firmes.

sterilize, to, neutralizar, esterilizar.

sterilized funds, fondos improductivos.

sterling

— area, zona esfera esterlina.

— balances, saldos de esterlinas.

— exchange, divisas en libra esterlina.

stock, (*n.*) acciones, existencias; (*v.*) almacenar.

— capital, capital social, acciones de capital.

— certificate, certificado de acciones.

—, **common,** acciones comunes, ordinarias.

— **company,** sociedad anónima, compañía por acciones.

— **control,** control de existencias.

— **dividend,** dividendo en acciones.

— **exchange,** bolsa de valores.

—, **in,** en existencia.

— **issue,** emisión de acciones.

— **market,** mercado, bolsa de valores.

—, **out of,** agotado.

— **speculation,** especulación, juego de bolsa.

— **ticker,** indicador de cotizaciones.

—, **to take,** hacerse el inventario.

— **trading,** juego de bolsa.

—, **voting,** acciones con derecho a voto.

stock-exchange quotations, cotizaciones, precios bursátiles.

stock-exchange securities, valores bursátiles.

stock-taking price, precio de inventario.

stock-turn, renovación de existencias, de inventario.

stockbroker, corredor de acciones.

stockholder, accionista.

stockjobber, corredor de bolsa.

stockowner, accionista.

stockpile, almacenamiento, almacenar reservas.

stop-loss order, orden de pérdida limitada, orden de compra o venta de acciones cuando la cotización pase de cierto límite.

stoppage, retención, suspensión, paro.

storage, almacenaje.

store, (*n.*) tienda, almacén; (*v.*) almacenar.

stores, provisiones, pertrechos.

stores ledger, libro de existencias.

stowage, estiba, bodega marítima.

straight B/L, conocimiento de embarque no endosable.

straight line depreciation, depreciación en línea recta.

strain, tensión, dificultad.

strata chart, diagrama de estratos.

strategic raw materials, materias primas estratégicas.

stratification after selection, estratificación posterior a la selección.

stratified sample, muestra estratificada.

stratify, to, estratificar.

street prices, precios fuera de bolsa.

strength of test, potencia de una prueba.

strike, huelga, paro.

strike in sympathy, huelga de solidaridad.

strikebreaker, rompehuelgas, esquirol.

strikes, riots and civil commotions clause, cláusula sobre huelgas, tumultos y disturbios civiles.

stringency, penuria, escasez monetaria.

sublease, subarriendo, subalquiler.

sublet, to, subarrendar, subalquilar.

subsample, submuestra.

subsampling, submuestreo.

subscription price, precio de emisión de nuevas acciones.

subsidiary company, compañía filial.

subsidiary ledger, auxiliar del (libro) mayor.

subsidize, to, subvencionar.

subsidy, subvención, subsidio.

—, production, subsidio a la producción.

subsistence, subsistencia.

— economy, economía de subsistencia.

— level, nivel de subsistencia.

— wages, salarios mínimos para subsistir.

substandard, subtipo, inferior.

substitute, sustituto, sustituir, sustitutivo.

substitutes, sucedáneos.

substitutive product, producto de sustitución, sucedáneo.

subtenant, subinquilino.

subunit, subunidad.

succession, sucesión.

— duties, impuestos de sucesión.

— tax, impuesto de sucesión.

sue, to, demandar, procesar.

summarize, to, resumir.

summary account, cuenta centralizadora.

sumptuary laws, leyes suntuarias.

sundries, artículos varios, gastos varios.

sundry expenses, gastos varios.

superannuated, incapacitado.

superannuation benefits, beneficios de jubilación.

superannuation fund, fondo de pensión.

superfluous, superfluo.

superimposed-curve chart, diagrama de curvas superpuestas.

supersede, to, sobreseer, reemplazar.

supervise, to, supervisar.

supplementary estimates, cálculos adicionales.

supplementary tax, impuesto adicional.

supplier, abastecedor.

supplies, abastecimientos.

supply, (*n.*) oferta; (*v.*) proveer.

— and demand, oferta y demanda.

— curve, curva de la oferta.

— price, precio de oferta.

support price, precio sostenido (por el gobierno).

surcharge, recargo, sobreprecio.

surety, caución, fianza.

surplus, superávit, excedente.

—, appraisal, superávit de revaluación.

—, book, superávit en libros.

—, capital, superávit de capital.

—, current, superávit disponible.

—, earned, superávit ganado.

— from consolidation, superávit de consolidación.

— funds, fondos sobrantes.

— stock, existencias sobrantes.

surrendered appropriations, créditos anulados.

surrender value, precio, valor de rescate.

surtax, recargo, sobretasa.

survey, estudio, encuesta.

survival, supervivencia.

suspend payment, to, suspender el pago.

suspense account, cuenta en suspenso.

swindle, (*n.*) estafa, (*v.*) estafar.

swindler, estafador.

swing of trade, fluctuación del mercado.

switch, to, cambiar, canjear.

symmetrical test, prueba simétrica.

sympathetic strike, huelga de solidaridad.

syndicate, sindicato.

system, sistema.

—, closed, sistema cerrado.

— of taxation, sistema fiscal.

—, open, sistema abierto.

systematic error, error constante.

systematic sampling, muestreo sistemático.

T

table of contents, índice.

tabulation of data, tabulación de datos.

take-home pay, sueldo neto, hechas todas las deducciones.

tangible assets, activo tangible.

tape price, precio de indicador automático (de acciones).

tare, tara.

— and tret, tara y merma.

tariff, tarifa, arancel.

— barriers, barreras arancelarias.

— nomenclature, nomenclatura arancelaria.

— protection, protección, arancelaria.

— union, unión, asociación de aduanas.

— war, guerra de tarifas, competencias entre dos o más naciones mediante tarifas selectivas.

tax, (*n.*) impuesto, contribución; (*v.*) gravar, imponer.

— administration, administración fiscal, fisco.

—, after, con los impuestos ya deducidos.

— allowance, rebaja del impuesto.

— barriers, barreras fiscales.

— base, base de impuesto, base imponible.

—, before, antes de deducir los impuestos.

— burden, gravamen fiscal.

— collection, recaudación fiscal.

— collector, recaudador fiscal.

— commision, agencia administrativa para recaudar impuestos.

— convention, convención fiscal.

— deduction, deducción, rebaja del impuesto.

— discrimination, discriminación fiscal.

— dodging, evasión de impuestos.

— equalization fund, fondo de estabilización de impuestos.

— evasion, evasión de impuestos.

— examiner, inspector fiscal.

— exemption, exención de impuestos.

— free income, ingreso libre de impuestos.

— free interest, intereses libres de impuestos.

— **gimmick,** malabarismo fiscal.

— **immunity,** inmunidad fiscal.

— **jurisdiction,** jurisdicción fiscal.

— **laws,** leyes fiscales.

— **list,** registro de contribuyentes.

— **on profits,** impuesto sobre utilidades.

— **policy,** política impositiva.

—, **property,** impuesto predial.

— **rate,** tasa, cuota de impuesto.

— **rebate,** bonificación fiscal.

— **reduction,** bonificación, reducción del impuesto.

— **refund,** devolución (parcial o total) del impuesto pagado.

— **report,** declaración de ingresos gravables.

— **return,** declaración de ingresos gravables.

— **revenue,** ingresos fiscales.

—, **sales,** impuesto sobre ingresos mercantiles.

— **selling,** venta con pérdida para lograr una disminución en los impuestos.

— **year,** año gravable, año fiscal.

tax-collector's office, administración de impuestos.

tax-exempt, exento o libre de impuestos.

taxable, gravable.

— **income,** ingreso gravable.

— **profits,** ganancias gravables.

— **value,** valor gravable.

— **year,** año fiscal.

taxation, imposición de impuestos.

taxpayer, contribuyente, causante.

technical training, preparación técnica.

technological unemployment, desempleo tecnológico (producido por la mecanización).

teller, cajero, pagador.

temporary, temporal.

— **annuity,** anualidad temporal.

— **investments,** inversiones transitorias.

— **migration,** migración temporal.

tenant, inquilino, arrendatario.

tender, propuesta, oferta.

—, **legal,** moneda de curso legal.

— **of payment,** oferta de pago.

tenure, tenencia, posesión.

term of patent, duración de una patente.

terminable annuity, anualidad temporal.

terminal wage, indemnización por despido.

terms of sale, condiciones de venta.

test, (*n.*) prueba, ensayo; (*v.*) probar, ensayar.

— **checks,** pruebas selectivas.

— **of random order,** prueba de orden aleatorio.

— **of records,** prueba de documentación y registros.

— **sample,** muestra para ensayo.

theoretical demography, demografía teórica.

theory of comparative costs, teoría de costos comparativos.

theory of international values, teoría de los valores internacionales.

thrift, economía, frugalidad.

through bill of lading, conocimiento de embarque directo (sin intervención de reembarcadores).

ticker, indicador de cotizaciones.

tied loan, préstamo condicionado.

tight money policy, política de restricción de créditos.

till money, efectivo de ventanilla.

time, tiempo.

— **antithesis,** antítesis cronológica.

— **bill,** letra a plazo.

— **budget,** tiempo estimado.

— **charter,** fletamiento por tiempo.

— **comparability factor,** factor de comparabilidad cronológica.

— **dependent random variable,** variable aleatoria cronológica dependiente.

— **deposits,** depósitos a plazo.

— **discounting,** descuento del futuro.

— **draft,** giro a plazo.

— **lag,** retardo, retraso.

— **letter of credit,** carta de crédito a plazo.

— **limit,** plazo.

— **limitation,** prescripción.

— **loan,** préstamo a plazo fijo.

— **of delivery,** plazo de entrega.

— **of departure,** hora de salida.

— **paper,** instrumentos de plazo fijo.

— **payments,** pagos a plazos.

— **policy,** póliza de tiempo.

— **series of prices,** serie cronológica de precios.

— **variance,** variación en tiempo.

— **wages,** salarios por hora.

title, título.

to-order B/L, conocimiento a la orden.

token payment, adelanto a cuenta de pago de una obligación.

tolerance factor, factor de tolerancia.

toll, (*n.*) peaje, impuesto por el uso de algo; (*v.*) pagar como peaje.

ton (long or gross) (gross tn.), tonelada (1016 kg).

ton (short or net) (tn. or net tn.), tonelada (907 kg).

tonnage, tonelaje.

tools, herramientas, medios.

top price, precio máximo.

top quality, calidad superior.

total, total.

— **amount,** importe total.

— **loss,** pérdida total.

— **product,** producto total.

— **receipts,** ingresos totales.

totalize, to, totalizar.

trade (*n.*) comercio; (*v.*) operar, comerciar.

— **acceptance,** aceptación comercial.

— **barriers,** barreras comerciales.

— **by barter,** comercio de trueque.

— **capital,** capital comercial.

— **controls,** restricciones al comercio.

— **cycle,** ciclo económico.

— **deficit,** balanza de pagos desfavorable.

— **discounts,** descuentos comerciales.

— **gap,** déficit económico comercial.

— **name,** marca de fábrica, razón social.

— **price,** precio corriente.

— **reporting,** información comercial.

— **system,** sistema comercial.

— **union,** sindicato.

— **usage,** costumbre del mercado.

trademark, marca de fábrica.

trading

— **account,** cuenta comercial.

— **corporation,** sociedad mercantil.

— **fund,** fondo comercial.

— **in futures,** operaciones de futuros.

training, adiestramiento, formación profesional.

transaction, negocio, transacción.

transactions motive, motivo transacción.

transfer, (*n.*) transferencia, traspaso; (*v.*) transladar.

transferable, transferible.

transhipment, transbordo.

transit duties, derechos de tránsito.

transit goods, mercancías en tránsito.

traveling expenses, gastos de viaje.

treasury, tesorería.

— **accounts,** cuentas de tesorería.

— **bonds,** bonos del estado, de la tesorería.

— **notes,** obligaciones del estado a corto plazo.

treaty, tratado, convenio.

trend, tendencia.

trial balance, balanza de prueba, de comprobación.

trimmed total fees, total de honorarios ajustados.

trust, fideicomiso, consorcio.

— **company,** compañía fiduciaria.

— **deposits,** depósitos especiales, en fideicomiso.

— **funds,** fondos fiduciarios.

turndown, rechazo.

turnover, rotación.

— **of inventories,** movimiento de existencias.

— **of labor,** cambios de personal.

— **tax,** impuesto sobre ingresos brutos.

typical business cycle, ciclo económico clásico.

U

unadjusted, no ajustado, pendiente.

unalloted balance, saldo no asignado.

unambiguous, inequívoco.

unappropriated, no asignado, no consignado.

unauthorized, no autorizado, desautorizado.

unavoidable loss, pérdidas inevitables.

unbalanced budget, presupuesto no nivelado.

uncertainty, incertidumbre.

unclaimed, sin reclamar, sin cobrar.

unclassified, no clasificado, sin clasificar.

uncollectable, incobrable, irrecuperable.

uncollected items, artículos no cobrados, por cobrar.

unconfirmed credit, crédito no confirmado.

uncovered, descubierto, en descubierto.

undated, sin fecha.

undeclared, no declarado.

undelivered, no entregado.

under

— **contract,** bajo contrato.

— **instructions,** con órdenes de.

— **protest,** bajo protesta.

— **way,** en camino, en curso.

underbid, to, hacer una propuesta más baja.

undercut, to, ofrecer mercancías a precios más bajos.

underdeveloped nations, países subdesarrollados.

underestimate, valuación, estimación baja.

underpaid, con sueldo insuficiente.

underpopulation, subpoblación.

underscore, to, subrayar.

undersell, to, vender a menor precio que, malbaratar.

undersigned, infrascrito, suscrito.

undersubscription, suscripción insuficiente.

undertake, to, emprender.

undertaking, compromiso, empresa.

undervalue, to, valuar en menos, estimar demasiado bajo.

underwrite, to, subscribir, asegurar.

underwriter, subscritor, compañía aseguradora.

underwriting contract, contrato de subscripción de valores.

undeveloped, no desarrollado, no explotado.

undistributed, no repartido.

undivided, no dividido, no repartido.

unearned, no ganado.

uneconomic, antieconómico.

unemployed, desocupado, cesante.

unemployment, desocupación, cesantía, desempleo.

— **benefits,** beneficios para desempleo.

— **compensation,** compensación por cesantía.

—, **frictional,** desocupación debida a resistencias.

— **insurance,** seguro de desocupación.

—, **involuntary,** desocupación involuntaria.

— **relief,** auxilio de desocupación.

unfair, injusto.

unfavorable, desfavorable.

— **balance of trade,** balanza comercial desfavorable, deficitaria.

unfeasible, impracticable.

unfit, incapaz, inhábil, impropio.

unforeseen expenses, gastos imprevistos, inesperados.

unfriendly, poco amistoso, desfavorable.

unfunded debt, deuda flotante, no consolidada.

ungraded, no clasificado.

unified mortgage, hipoteca consolidada.

unilateral legislation, leyes unilaterales.

unincorporated, no incorporado.

union, sindicato, gremio obrero.

— labor, trabajadores sindicalizados.

— shop, empresa en la que el patrón puede emplear obreros sindicalizados o no, pero con la condición de que los no sindicalizados se sindicalicen dentro de un plazo fijo.

— wage, salario sindical.

unionize, to, agremiar, agremiarse.

unit

— cost, costo unitario.

— inventory, inventario por unidades.

— price, precio unitario.

— value index, índice de valores unitarios.

— weight, peso unitario.

unlawful, ilegal.

unlicensed, no autorizado.

unlimited, ilimitado, sin límite.

unliquidated, no liquidado.

— damages, daños no liquidados.

— debt, deuda no determinada o por pagar.

unlisted securities, valores no inscritos en la bolsa.

unmarketable, incomerciable.

unnegotiable, innegociable.

unofficial, extraoficial.

unpaid, sin pagar, por pagar.

unpopulated area, área despoblada.

unpredictable, incierto, imposible de predecir.

unproductive, improductivo.

unprofitable, antieconómico.

unrated company, compañía no clasificada.

unrefundable, no restituible.

unsinkable debt, deuda no amortizable.

unskilled labor, trabajadores no clasificados, no especializados.

unsound securities, valores especulativos.

unstable, inestable.

— process, proceso inestable.

unstated, no declarado.

unsuitable, inapropiado.

unwarranted, no garantizado, injustificado.

unweighted index, índice no ponderado.

upkeep, conservación.

upset price, precio mínimo fijado en una subasta.

upswing, aumento, alza, mejora (de precios).

upturn, aumento, alza mejora (de precios).

urban-rural population, población urbana rural.

usage, costumbre, usanza.

usance, plazo a que se debe pagar una letra de cambio.

use tax, impuesto sobre utilización de bienes.

user, usuario, consumidor.

— cost, costo de uso.

usury, usura.

utility, utilidad, empresa de servicio público.

utopian, utópico.

V

vagueness, vaguedad.

validate, validar, legalizar.

value, (*n.*) valor; (*v.*) valorar, valuar, estimar, tasar.

— added, valor agregado.

— agreed upon, valor entendido.

—, appraised, valor estimado, de avalúo.

—, assessed, valor catastral.

— at factor cost, valor al costo de los factores.

— at maturity, valor al vencimiento.

—, book, valor en libros.

—, cost, valor de costo.

—, depreciated, valor depreciado.

—, face, valor nominal.

— for collection, valor al cobro.

— for customs purposes, valor en arancel aduanal, en tarifa aduanal.

—, going, valor de negocio en marcha.

— in account, valor en cuenta.

—, intangible, valor intangible.

—, junk, valor de desecho.

—, liquidation, valor de liquidación.

—, market, valor de mercado.

—, par, valor a la par.

— received, valor recibido.

— retained, valor retenido.

— secured, valor en prenda, en garantía.

— sound, valor justo.

—, surrender, valor de rescate.

vanishing point, punto de desvanecimiento.

variable, variable.

— **annuity,** anualidad variable.

— **budget,** presupuesto variable.

— **burden,** gastos variables.

variable-yield debenture, obligación de ingresos variables.

variance from the average, variación del promedio.

varying-interval prediction, pronóstico a intervalos variables.

vector random variable, variable vectorial aleatoria.

vendor, vendedor.

venture, empresa, especulación, riesgo.

verify, to, verificar.

vertical expansion, expansión vertical.

vested interests, intereses creados.

vested rights, derechos adquiridos.

veto, (*n.*) veto; (*v.*) vetar; prohibir.

visible balance of trade, balanza visible de comercio.

visible items of trade, exportaciones e importaciones de mercancías.

vital statistics, estadísticas vitales, demográficas.

voided check, cheque anulado.

volume discount, descuento por volumen.

volume of employment, volumen de ocupación.

vote, (*n.*) voto; (*v.*) votar.

— **by proxy,** voto o votar por poder.

— **of confidence,** voto de confianza.

vouch, to, comprobar, certificar.

voucher, comprobante de pago, justificante.

W

wage, jornal, salario, pago, sueldo.

— **bargains,** convenios sobre salarios.

— **board,** junta, comisión de sueldos.

— **dispute,** controversia sobre salarios.

— **earner,** asalariado.

— **freeze,** congelación de sueldos.

— **goods,** mercancías para asalariados, artículos en que se gastan los salarios.

—, **money,** salario nominal.

— **policy,** política en materia de salarios.

— **rate,** tasa de salarios.

—, **real,** salario real.

— **scale,** tabulador de sueldos.

— **units,** unidades de salario.

waiver, renuncia.

walkout, huelga, paro.

want, (*n.*) necesidad, carencia; (*v.*) necesitar.

— **of balance,** desequilibrio.

—, **to be in,** estar necesitado.

war economy, sistema económico en tiempo de guerra.

war indemnity payments, indemnizaciones de guerra.

warehouse, almacén, depósito, bodega.

— **receipt,** recibo de almacén.

warrant, (*n.*) vale, certificado de depósito, garantía; (*v.*) garantizar, avalar.

wash sale, venta ficticia.

wash-up time, tiempo pagado para lavarse.

wastage, desgaste, desperdicio.

waste, (*n.*) desperdicio; (*v.*) desperdiciar.

— **control,** control de desperdicios.

— **money, to,** malgastar el dinero.

— **product,** producto de desecho.

wasteful, antieconómico.

watered stock, capital inflado.

waybill, hoja de ruta, guía aérea.

weaken, to, debilitarse.

wealth-owning class, clases propietarias de riquezas.

wear and tear, desgaste, depreciación.

weight, peso, coeficientede ponderación.

weighted, ponderado.

— **arithmetic mean,** media aritmética ponderada.

— **average,** promedio ponderado.

— **geometric mean,** media geométrica ponderada.

— **harmonic mean,** media armónica ponderada.

— **index,** índice ponderado.

— **value,** valor ponderado.

weighting, ponderación.

welfare, bienestar social, asistencia pública, previsión social.

— **fund,** fondo de previsión social.

— **work,** prestaciones asistenciales.

well-being, bienestar.

wetbacks, espaldas mojadas.
wharf, muelle, embarcadero.
wholesale, mayoreo, venta al por mayor.
— **market,** mercado al por mayor.
— **prices,** precios de mayoreo, por mayor.
— **trade,** comercio al por mayor.
wholesaler, mayorista.
wildcat strike, huelga no sancionada por el sindicato.
willingness, buena disposición.
windfall gain, ganancias imprevistas.
windfall loss, pérdidas imprevistas.
withdraw, to, retirar, retirarse.
— **cash, to,** retirar efectivo.
— **from calculation, to,** retirar de la circulación.
withdrawals, retiros de fondos.
withheld, retenido.
withhold at the source, to, retener (los impuestos) en el origen.
work, (*n.*) trabajo; (*v.*) trabajar.
— **at a loss, to,** trabajar con pérdidas.
— **done,** trabajo realizado.
— **in process,** manufactura en proceso.

— **load,** faena.
workable, viable.
workday, día laborable.
working
— **assets,** activo circulante.
— **balance,** saldo corriente.
— **capital,** capital en giro, activo circulante.
— **capital fund,** fondo de operación.
— **class,** clase obrera.
— **control,** control efectivo.
— **day,** día laborable.
— **expenses,** gastos de explotación.
— **force,** personal obrero.
— **hours,** horas laborables.
— **index,** índice adecuado, índice de guía.
— **papers,** papeles de trabajo.
— **partner,** socio activo.
— **program,** programa de trabajo.
— **reserve,** reservas de operación.
— **tools,** equipo individual de trabajo.
workmen's compensation, compensación por accidentes de trabajo.
worksaving, economía de trabajo.
workshop, taller.
worsening, evolución desfavorable.

worth, valor, valía.
—, net, valor neto.
—, present, valor actual.
worthless, inútil, sin valor.
write, to, escribir.
— in, to, intercalar, insertar.

— off, to, anular, eliminar.
write-off, cargo por depreciación.
written, escrito.
— agreement, acuerdo por escrito.

Y

yard (yd), yarda (0.9144 m).
year-end dividend, dividendo de fin de año.
yearly income, ingreso anual.
yearly adjustment, ajuste anual.
yellow-dog contract, promesa del obrero de no sindicalizarse.

yield, (*n.*) rendimiento, producto; (*v.*) redituar, producir.
— basis, tasación según rendimiento.
— rate, tipo de rendimiento.
— to maturity, rendimiento al vencimiento.
yielding, productivo.

Z

zone, (*n.*) zona; (*v.*) dividir en zonas.

zoning, zonificación, planeación de zonas.

192

Appendix

Weights and Measures

Pesas y Medidas

Metric and English Equivalents

Linear Measure

millimeter (mm)	milímetro	(0.0393 in.)
centimeter (cm)	centímetro	(0.3937 in.)
decimeter (dm)	decímetro	(3.937 in.)
meter (m)	metro	(3.28 ft)
decameter (dam)	decámetro	(32.8 ft)
hectometer (hm)	hectómetro	(328.08 ft)
kilometer (km)	kilómetro	(1093.6 yd)
inch (in.)	pulgada	(2.54 cm)
foot (ft)	pie	(30.48 cm)
yard (yd)	yarda	(91.44 cm)
mile (land) (mi)	milla terrestre	(1609.3 m)
mile (nautical) (mi)	milla marítima	(1852 m)

Weights

milligram (mg)	miligramo	(0.015 gr.)
centigram (cg)	centigramo	(0.154 gr.)
decigram (dg)	decigramo	(1.54 gr.)
gram (g)	gramo	(0.0352 avdp. oz)
decagram (dag.)	decagramo	(0.3527 avdp. oz)
hectogram (hg)	hectogramo	(3.527 avdp. oz)
kilogram (kg)	kilogramo	(2.2046 avdp. lb.)

grain (gr)	grano	(64.799 mg)
ounce (avoirdupois) (oz avdp.)	onza avoirdupois	(28.35 g)
ounce (troy) (oz t.)	onza troy	(31.1 g)
pound (avoirdupois) (lb avdp.)	libra	(453.59 g)
ton (long or gross) (U.K.)	tonelada	(2240 lb avdp.) (1016 kg)
ton (short or net) (U.S.)	tonelada	(2000 lb avdp.) (907.18 kg)
ton (metric)	tonelada métrica	(2204.62 lb avdp.) (1000 kg)

Liquid Measure

milliliter (ml)	mililitro	(0.0338 fl. oz)
centiliter (cl)	centilitro	(0.338 fl. oz)
deciliter (dl)	decilitro	(3.3814 fl. oz)
liter (l.)	litro	(1.056 qt)
decaliter (dal.)	decalitro	(10.56 qt)
hectoliter (hl)	hectolitro	(105.67 qt)
kiloliter (kl)	kilolitro	(1056.7 qt)
ounce (fluid) (fl. oz)	onza	(U.S. 29.57 ml) (U.K. 28.41 ml)
pint (pt)	pinta	(U.S. 0.473 l.) (U.K. 0.568 l.)
quart (qt)	cuarto de galón	(U.S. 0.946 l.) (U.K. 1.13 l.)
gallon (gal)	galón	(U.S. 3.785 l.) (U.K. 4.546 l.)

Square Measure

square millimeter (mm²)	milímetro cuadrado	(0.00155 in²)
square centimeter (cm²)	centímetro cuadrado	(0.1550 in²)
square decimeter (dm²)	decímetro cuadrado	(15.50 in²)
square meter (m²)	metro cuadrado	(1.1960 yd²)
area (a)	área	(119 yd²) (100 m²)
hectare (ha)	hectárea	(11,960 yd²) (10,000 m²)
square kilometer (km)	kilómetro cuadrado	(0.38608 mi²)
square inch (in²)	pulgada cuadrada	(6.45 cm²)
square foot (ft²)	pie cuadrado	(9.29 dm²)
square yard (yd²)	yarda cuadrada	(0.836 m²)
acre	acre (4,840 yd²)	(0.4047 ha.)
hectare (ha)	hectárea	(10,000 m²)
square mile (mi²)	milla cuadrada	(2.59 km²)

Cubic Measure

cubic centimeter (cm³)	centímetro cúbico	(0.061 in³)
cubic decimeter (dm³)	decímetro cúbico	(61.023 in³)
cubic meter (m³)	metro cúbico	(35.315 ft³)
cubic inch (in³)	pulgada cúbica	(16.387 cm³)
cubic foot (ft³)	pie cúbico	(28.317 dm³)
cubic yard (yd³)	yarda cúbica	(0.764 m³)

Numbers/Números

1	one	uno, una
2	two	dos
3	three	tres
4	four	cuatro
5	five	cinco
6	six	seis
7	seven	siete
8	eight	ocho
9	nine	nueve
10	ten	diez
11	eleven	once
12	twelve	doce
13	thirteen	trece
14	fourteen	catorce
15	fifteen	quince
16	sixteen	dieciseis
17	seventeen	diecisiete
18	eighteen	dieciocho
19	nineteen	diecinueve
20	twenty	veinte
21	twenty-one	veintiuno
22	twenty-two	veintidos
23	twenty-three	veintitres
24	twenty-four	veinticuatro
25	twenty-five	veinticinco
26	twenty-six	veintiseis
27	twenty-seven	veintisiete
28	twenty-eight	veintiocho
29	twenty-nine	veintinueve
30	thirty	treinta

31	thirty-one	treinta y uno
40	forty	cuarenta
50	fifty	cincuenta
60	sixty	sesenta
70	seventy	setenta
80	eighty	ochenta
90	ninety	noventa
100	one hundred	cien
101	one hundred and one	ciento uno, -a
200	two hundred	doscientos, -as
201	two hundred and one	doscientos uno, -a
300	three hundred	trescientos, -as
400	four hundred	cuatrocientos, -as
500	five hundred	quinientos, -as
600	six hundred	seiscientos, -as
700	seven hundred	setecientos, -as
800	eight hundred	ochocientos, -as
900	nine hundred	novecientos, -as
1000	one thousand	mil
1001	one thousand and one	mil uno, -una
2000	two thousand	dos mil
10,000	ten thousand	diez mil
100,000	one hundred thousand	cien mil
200,000	two hundred thousand	doscientos mil
1,000,000	one million	un millón
1,000,000,000	U.K. one billion U.S. one thousand million	mil millones